ANCIENT JUDAISM AND MODERN CATEGORY-FORMATION

"Judaism," "Midrash," "Messianism," and Canon
in the Past Quarter-Century

Studies in Judaism

ANCIENT JUDAISM AND MODERN CATEGORY-FORMATION

"Judaism," "Midrash," "Messianism," and Canon
in the Past Quarter-Century

Jacob Neusner

UNIVERSITY
PRESS OF
AMERICA

LANHAM • NEW YORK • LONDON

Copyright © 1986 by

University Press of America,® Inc.

4720 Boston Way
Lanham, MD 20706

3 Henrietta Street
London WC2E 8LU England

Library of Congress Cataloging-in-Publication Data

Neusner, Jacob, 1932-
    Ancient Judaism and modern category formation.

    (Studies in Judaism)
    Includes index.
    1. Judaism—History—To 70 A.D.—Historiography.
2. Midrash—History and criticism. 3. Messiah—History
of doctrines. I. Title. II. Series.
BM170.N455 1986   296'.09'01   85-30416
ISBN 0-8191-5395-8 (alk. paper)
ISBN 0-8191-5396-6 (pbk. : alk. paper)

All University Press of America books are produced on acid-free
paper which exceeds the minimum standards set by the National
Historical Publications and Records Commission.

For

JASON BOGART SMITH

in celebration of his
becoming a
bar mitzvah

and for his parents
and sister

Jonathan Z. Smith
Elaine Smith
and
Siobhan Smith

on the same happy occasion

Though not quite present at the creation,
I know that this particular
category
is well formed indeed .

Now on to the huppah !

CONTENTS

CONTENTS

Preface

In this book I propose to investigate the categories that commonly serve for the description, analysis, and interpretation of ancient Judaism and the principles that form those categories. This I do in Chapters One, Two, and Three. I further propose, in Chapter Four, a new basis for category-formation. It is one that proceeds inductively and descriptively, with primary focus on the canon and its replication of one social reality, not deductively and theologically, as at present, with focus on statements of belief, philosophically construed. For at issue when we study a religion is not principally what people believe and the inner structure of their ideas, though that matter proves mildly interesting. Rather, what we need to find out is the relationship between what people believed and what they did, and, more significantly, the way of life that they worked out and the world-view that they developed in accounting for that way of life: their social being.

For the study of religion involves knowledge, not merely belief and feeling and sensibility. It is public and produces reasoned discourse about matters of fact and interpretation, like any other field of learning. And that is because of the public character of religion, its power as a fact of human life both then and now. The center of religion lies not in the mind, in here, but in society, out there, so I maintain. Hence category-formation begins in an inductive process of inquiry into the things people do together, as a group, as a society, as a nation, rather than the things people believe, one by one or in unison. And one of the most important things people do together is venerate holy books, writing them, copying them, preserving them, quoting them, interpreting them, in all, building their social lives as a group in constant response to what they find, or think they find, in the canon that contains their world view and instructions for their way of life. Religion as the world knows it forms the ground of social being, the foundation for politics and economic behavior, the definitive force in the shaping of culture, the center of the unfolding life of individuals, the bond for the community. These are things we can study. We study them in the data produced by religion, which, for the period in question, is defined by the canon, the holy books of Judaism. The canon is what preserves religion in all literate religions. That is why religion accounts for the condition of much of the world today and most of it in times past and the canon is the place at which to begin studying that powerful force in human life and history. If, therefore, we propose to study religion, we had best start our work where religion makes the difference, which is, to begin with, in society, as a system encompassing all things, and only by the way, also in the construction of intellectual compositions.

Categories, as I said, dictate the intellectual processes of learning and so determine understanding: what we choose to learn, how we proceed to explain and make sense of it. As to description, the category *Judaism* defines what we study. That category tells us what we collect and what we do not collect, how we arrange what we have assembled and so construe the relationships among data deemed Judaic. As to analysis, for the purpose of making sense of our data once described, we compare and contrast among groups of data. We seek perspective on one thing by comparing it to other things of its class. That forms the foundation of any analytical, not merely descriptive, initiative. It is *midrash* that, in the study of ancient Judaism, makes possible categorical comparison and contrast, on the basis of which all analysis rests. That is why I choose *midrash* and what is called *comparative midrash* for my discussion of an analytical category, but others may find different analytical categories for suggestive examination. As to interpretation, we interpret what we have described and analyzed by asking about the purpose and goal of the whole: the sense of the data seen all together, the intent and plan of it all viewed all at once. Accordingly, for Judaism the category *Messianism*, sets forth the teleology of the subject of our study, hence the correct route and strategy for interpreting it.

These then form the categories under study in this book. The category-formations subject to analysis here tell us how to select and organize whatever information we propose to classify as Judaic. The categories *Judaism, Messianism,* and *midrash* define the sense and proportion, the harmony and the balance, telling us what matters, how and where and why what matters makes a difference. Accordingly, if we wish to attain a clear understanding of the way in which we form data into intelligible patterns of description and so define, out of masses of information, the limits of our subject in particular, we examine operative categories: hence category-formation.

The organization of the book then is simple: description then becomes possible through the category, *Judaism.* In Chapter One we deal with the category, *Judaism.* Analysis we carry on through processes of comparison and contrast of data, e.g., data common to several Judaisms or to one of those Judaisms and a Christianity, hence in Chapter Two we take up comparative *midrash.* Interpretation we accomplish through the inquiry into teleology, hence *Messianism.* In Chapter Three we turn to the category, *Messianism.* How useful is that category? We find that it serves precisely as well as does Judaism, and for exactly the same reason. In Chapter Three I am able to propose a test for the suitability or uselessness of a category and to carry out that test on "the Messianism" of "Judaism." So the work of description, analysis, and interpretation depends upon the three category-formations at hand. And we can begin to test our categories and to see whether or not they meet reasonable criteria.

My purpose is to argue that all of them violate the inner composition of the data they are employed to classify. For all three constitute intellectual, not social constructs. The categories are formed in error, namely, by deduction from philosophical processes. So they generate constructions that distort the data subject to categorization. In Chapter Four I spell out what I believe to be the correct principle of category-formation for the study of Judaism(s). The principle of generating or forming categories derive from an inductive analysis of the evidence at hand, as I shall spell out as best I can. My proposed principle of category-formation derives from the categories defined by the canon of the religion under study. Let me with emphasis state the thesis of the book as a whole:

The canon forms the correct principle of category-formation for the study of Judaisms through description, analysis, and interpretation of systems. The categories generated by the canon then require the description of the canon's several components, one by one, the analysis of the relationship, revealed through comparison and contrast, of one component with another, and the interpretation of how all the components of the canon come together to form a single cogent system. That system then comes under description through the consideration of the autonomy of each component, the connections among the several components, the continuity among all of the components to form a whole and cogent statement: a religion..

This point emerges in every chapter, but with special force in Chapters Two and Four, which are the more constructive essays, rather than in Chapters One and Three, which aim at showing the difficulties posed to us by the available categories.

So my main point is simple. Context dictates contents, and categories define context. Out of context facts present gibberish, in context, insight and meaning. Out of context information is useless -- a telephone number to a house where we no one is home. In context information matters. And in this book category is a concrete term for context. By category-formation, then, I mean the way in which we determine what we want to know and how we propose to organize the facts we seek.

In this book I carry forward the reflections of Robert D. Baird,[1] who treats as equivalent the labor of definition and that of category-formation. He therefore defines definition as he works out the ways in which historians of religion define their categories and so determine what data fall into the classification of religion: "thereby marking the limits and extent of his study.,"[2] Baird therefore asks historians of religion to make explicit the definition of what it is that they

---

[1]Robert D. Baird, Category *Formation and the History of Religions* (The Hague and Paris, 1971: Mouton) pp. 1-16.

[2] *ibid.*, p. 2.

study, reviewing types of definitions and categorizing the actual definitions that operate in the field. His main point is this:

A real definition points to acquiring knowledge about things. Such definitions are not only true or false but presumably come at the end of a study. One also expects some form of proof. It is inconceivable that a functional definition should come at the end of a book, since it determines how an otherwise ambiguous words will be used. But a discussion of the nature of the thing to which a word unambiguously refers could only come after an analysis of that thing.[3]   Since, Baird notes, religion does not refer to any one thing, problems of defining religion multiply: "it either includes too much or too little in terms of universal usage." In choosing, among Baird's alternatives, *category-formation* rather than *definition*, I seek a broader frame of reference. What I want to study, as I have explained, is how, in the description of ancient Judaism, we know what we want to know. When we can specify the categories among which we organize naked facts and explain the formation of those categories, we gain an articulate and conscious picture of how, in our own minds, we turn facts into knowledge, knowledge into insight, so gaining understanding of our subject.

For knowledge is not the same thing as acquiring facts, and, indeed, merely knowing, out of all context, one detail or another guarantees we shall misinterpret everything we think we know. Gibberish turns into knowledge when words follow rules of syntax. Facts become learning when intellectual rules come into play. Upon that premise this book lays forth its propositions.

Readers require no reminder that the writer does not claim to practice philosophy of religion. I am a working historian of religion, and no more than that. Out of my work I have had to solve certain problems left over for me by philosophers of religion, as they go on to their own work. I do not mean to move about the boundaries of their field. At the same time, by their emphasis on system and order in ideas, they have obscured the deeper system and order in the sources that contain (among many other things) those ideas and so attest to a religious system -- world view, way of life, addressed to a distinctive social group. Those sources constitute the canon, and, as I shall propose here, the canon forms the original and generative category -- that above all.

Jacob Neusner

Program in Judaic Studies
Brown University
Providence, Rhode Island U.S.A.

October 10, 1985
25 Tishre 5746

---

[3] *ibid.*, p. 11.

Acknowledgements

This book began twenty-one years ago at Dartmouth College in discussions with Abraham J. Karp. I had then been teaching in a Department of Religion for two years and had begun to wonder what I teach when I teach about Judaism. What troubled me was that I could not explain what Judaism is and is not: why teach this, not that? I did not know how to describe a Judaism. So I pursued the issue with Abraham Karp and in these discussions reached the conclusion, which I have maintained ever since, that there really is no such thing as Judaism. That word stands for the reification of something I still cannot identify. So I began to reflect on the category at hand, that is, the *-ism* and the *ism* -izing of something that is not an *-ism* at all, and then I reflected on categories in general, and finally, I wondered about category-formation -- hence, this book. It is a simple effort, and I suspect rather unsophisticated. But it is critical to my work and the best I can do, and I wanted to share my approaches and ideas for colleagues' comment.

My earliest efforts to find a solution to the problem took shape in what became *The Way of Torah: An Introduction to Judaism,* which, through successive editions, has served as a vehicle for the practical expression of the results of an on-going exercise in theory. My most current effort will take form in *From Testament to Torah: An Introduction to Judaism* . This book explains the theory behind that text-book -- which is, of course, the cutting edge of theory, as teaching always brings us to the outer edge of our learning. So if the academic study of religion followed the paths I should want to explore, a different sort of text-book may lead students into the study of the most important subject in the curriculum: the reason why the world is what it is, which is, religion. A Judaism is a religion. We require theories of how systems of religion -- way of life, world view, addressed to a particular social group -- take shape where and when they do. Why do they work when they work, and why do they lose the quality of self-evidence when people cease to find their teachings and demands self-evident? This we must learn, if we hope to understand humanity then and now and tomorrow.

Still, that is a separate question, and focuses on a problem that, in my present academic circumstance, I do not have to solve. Those who do do not grasp the problem at all: they are failed philosophers or theologians manqué -- when they are not merely making things up as they go along and calling the result the study of religion, or, even, of a religion. But some do no more than that.

I had the advantage of extensive discussions of the plan of this book and its thesis with William Scott Green, University of Rochester. My colleague Ernest S. Frerichs contributed much, but, especially, (along with his wife, as well as my wife and two of our children) his company on a trip to New Zealand and Australia, and his willingness to share my interest in the Maori and the Pakeha as an example of encounter between two "others."

This book contains both fresh materials and also substantial revisions of earlier writings.

Preface: all new

Introduction: all new

Chapter One: I have made use of materials of the first version of my preface for *Judaisms and their Messiahs* (Cambridge, 1986: Cambridge University Press) and of my lecture, "The Theological Enemies of Religious Studies." Both have been substantially revised and recast.

Chapter Two: I have extensively revised and reworked passages in my *Comparative Midrash: The Plan and Program of Genesis Rabbah and Leviticus Rabbah* (Atlanta, 1985: Scholars Press for Brown Judaic Studies), in particular the Preface and Appendix of that book. The focus is the same, however, namely, analysis as an exercise in comparison and contrast: first, the problem of defining, then the issue of comparing what we have defined. That problem is exemplified by the questions, what is Midrash, and what do we do when we compare Midrash to Midrash? In the present context the relevance is clear.

Chapter Three: I have revised and recast "One Theme, Two Settings. The Messiah in the Literature of the Synagogue and in the Rabbis' Canon of Late Antiquity," in *Major Trends in Formative Judaism. Second Series. Texts, Contents, and Contexts* (Chico, 1984: Scholars Press for Brown Judaic Studies), pp. 73-98. At issue is whether we can define "*the* Messianic Doctrine in Judaism," as various scholars have maintained in writing books by such a title, and, if we can, then what data determine the doctrine of Judaism, what data do not, and how we are to tell the difference. That issue serves for the present work as well, so the revisions are not so extensive as in the other chapters.

Chapter Four: I have revised and rewritten small pieces of "Anthropology and the Study of Talmudic Literature," which served as the Samuel Friedland Lecture, The Jewish Theological Seminary of America Academic Convocation at Miami Beach, February 28, 1979, and was circulated also by JTSA to the Rabbinical Assembly, and which, in revised form appeared in *Method and Meaning in Ancient Judaism* (Missoula, 1979: Scholars Press for Brown Judaic Studies), pp. 21-40. And, as in the case of Chapter Two, I have extensively revised and reworked some passages in my *Comparative Midrash: The Plan and Program of Genesis Rabbah and Leviticus Rabbah* (Atlanta, 1985: Scholars Press for Brown Judaic Studies), in particular the Appendix of that book.

Introduction

How Categories Take Shape and Why They Matter

Even the name, Maori, is an abstraction, created in the nineteenth century

M. P. K. Sorrenson

The principle of category-formation tells us how we know what we want to know and, therefore, also how to find it out. Here I explain how in the study of religion at present we decide what we want to know about ancient Judaism and find it out. Because I devote my life to the description, analysis, and interpretation of the writings produced by Judaic sages in the first seven centuries A.D., I take up the Judaism that took shape in those centuries in the Land of Israel ("Palestine") and in Babylonia, and have defined matters ever since. I seek to produce an articulate statement concerning the categories of my field, which I believe are asymmetrical to the sources, and the correct way in which to form them, hence the title of this book: category-formation in the study of ancient Judaism. When we understand the categories we use for the selection and organization of information, we can make better sense of our studies. Then we not only do them, we also explain them. When, moreover, we can account for the formation of our categories, we gain insight into the structure and composition of our subject: not only what we know, but why and how we know it.

I

Description, Analysis, Interpretation

When we propose to gather data and sort out those data into intelligible patterns by public and shared rules, we engage in three processes of intellect. We describe the data, we analyze them, then we interpret what we have described. All public work of social study requires these three processes of mind.

The category that tells us how to *describe*, therefore to define, our subject is *Judaism*. When we study *Judaism*, we collect data we regard as probative for that category and omit data we regard as irrelevant to that category. Therefore *Judaism* tells us what, and by the way, how to describe: the subject at hand. I argue that that is the wrong subject.

The category that explains to us one important way in which to *analyze* our subject is, *Midrash*. *Midrash* refers to exegesis of the Hebrew Scriptures. As I shall explain in Chapter Two, it defines a category that commonly serves to establish the framework for comparison and contrast of data within our subject. For people write articles and books in the field they correctly call *comparative Midrash*. I shall argue that they compare the wrong things when they compare *midrash* [es].

Finally, *Messianism* is a category that provides us with a perspective for the *interpretation* of our subject. Since the category *Judaism* homogenizes all data, the category *Messianism* generates statements --- books or articles -- of or on *The Messianic Idea in Judaism*. Considering the category, *Messianism*, therefore permits us to test the entire system resting on the generative category, *Judaism*. These interpretative statements, I shall show, obscure important traits of the data and therefore do not pass a simple test of verification or falsification. I simply take the data on which people commonly rely in describing the Messianic Idea of Judaism and perform a simple test. I read them item by item, describing each set in turn. The upshot? When we join together all data into a single doctrine, e.g., the Messianism of Judaism, we end up misinterpreting traits of the data. But when we differentiate among our data, e.g., by contextual variables, then we are able to observe and distinguish traits in the data. So when we do things wrong, we miss important points of observation. And when we do them right, we see things we otherwise would not see. On that basis, I argue, the category itself proves inappropriate to the data. And if that result is so of *the Messianic idea* of *Judaism*, it also applies to *Judaism*. So we pursue the analyses of categories and their formation in Chapters One through Three.

At the end, in Chapter Four, I offer an argument in behalf of a different mode of category-formation, I mean, an alternative way of forming our definitive category, and, it follows, also an alternative category. On the basis of the principle of category formation I propose, an entirely fresh reading of the data -- description, analysis through comparison and contrast, and interpretation, will emerge. In fact, I have been pursuing precisely the mode of category-formation I advocate here, and I wrote this book so as to explain what, in many other books, I have been doing for twenty-five years.[1] So I mean to analyze existing categories and offer a way to form new ones.

Let me now spell out what is at issue in the formation of the received categories. Three categories predominate when we propose to describe *Judaism*,[2] telling us, as I said, what we wish to know, and how we shall find it out. These

---

[1] The companion-volume, *Ancient Judaism and Contemporary Fundamentalism* (Atlanta, 1986: Scholars Press for Brown Judaic Studies), explains why I think what others have been doing for the same twenty-five years is hopelessly wrong in fundamental premise as to the character and use of evidence -- therefore worthless in result, except for occasional details.

[2] In italics a word refers to a category, not in italics, it is generic. I refer now to *Judaism* as a category, and so throughout with *Midrash* and *Messianism*. The *-ism* of Juda*ism* and of Messian*ism* provide the same indication.

are the category just now introduced, *Judaism*, and two others, the one governing how the links of society and chains of culture are described, namely, *Midrash*, accounting for the continuity of culture, and the other, *Messianism*, the doctrine of this same *Judaism* that accounts for the purpose of the system. So in the three received categories we define a system, account for its coherence, and explain its purpose and direction. To state matters as they presently are framed: *Judaism*, the fundamental organizing classification, constitutes a coherent category, a body of doctrine, beginning to the present, because of the power of *Midrash* to establish connections from beginnings in Scripture to doctrines and beliefs today, and because of the power of *Messianism* to impart meaning and purpose to the whole: these three, definition, coherence, teleology.

Are there no alternatives? For some lay claim in behalf of the intellectual system at hand -- definition, method, purpose -- on the authority of self-evidence, the universal acknowledgement accorded by common sense. How else -- they ask -- select and organize data, finding its points of cogency and its method of continuity, its teleological dimension, than by the categories, *Judaism*, *Midrash*, *Messianism*? They maintain that these are the obvious categories, based on the only rational formative process, which is, common sense.

Let me violate all rules of rational discourse to show the contrary. Specifically, I shall argue from an anecdote. Why adduce a mere anecdote in evidence in a serious argument? Because people think the present categories, beginning with Judaism, self-evident. There is no other. But as I shall now suggest, there is nothing self-evident about them. If I can point to one instance, plausible on the face of it, in which the present category-formation does *not* prove self-evident, then choices open up. Nothing any longer may then demand the status of mere common sense. Why not? Because of the very character of a claim of self-evidence. For something to prove self-evident it must commonly make sense. A plausible exception, therefore, forms an insuperable obstacle, just as much as does a single exception to the claim of uniqueness. That is, if I claim something is unique, then nothing else can form part of its species, or even its genus. Once we can find a plausible counterpart or parallel or equivalent, then what is alleged to be unique no longer is unique. To cite anecdotal evidence then constitutes a valid mode of argument against claims of self-evidence and common sense, just as a single exceptional case invalidates the claim of uniqueness.

As to plausible categories other than the received ones, therefore, I invoke the case to come. My exception comes to me from my grandmother.[3] My

---

[3] I choose my grandmother because, in discourse among scholars on the definition and character of Judaism, a fair number of colleagues, specializing in subjects other than in the study of Judaism, or in aspects of Jewish data other than the study of religion, invoke arguments from what their parents or grandparents or rabbis happened to tell them. So what my bubbee told me forms a valid counter-argument in the court of I-think-you-think.

grandmother, who spoke Yiddish and came from near Koretz, in White Russia, provides the unanswerable argument. She did not use the word we use when speaking of the things of which we speak when we wish to speak of when we say, *Judaism*. She used a different word, which in fact referred to different things, and her category of definition, serving as does the category, *Judaism*, to refer to the whole, all in all, taken all together, therefore instructed her to speak of different things. Her categories and ours, which refer to the same data in the same social world, in fact encompass different data from those taken in by ours in our speaking, categorically, of *Judaism*. So do different categories imposed on the same corpus of facts turn out to organize different worlds in different ways. The difference? When my grandmother wished to invoke a category that included everything all together and in correct proportion, she used the word-category, *Torah* -- as did many centuries of Jews before her. Her category fell into the classification of symbol, that is, a symbol that in itself encompassed the whole of the system that the category at hand was meant to describe. Our category, by contrast, does not invoke an encompassing symbol but a system of thought, as I shall explain presently. So today for an equivalent sentence, we resort to the word-category, *Judaism*. And, in fact, the two categories do not correspond, though, meant to function in the same way, they run parallel to one another. So *Torah* as a category serves as a symbol, everywhere present in detail and holding all the details together.[4] *Judaism* as a category serves as a statement of the main points: the intellectual substrate of it all. If we uncover no such uniform substrate, we have problems -- unless we use our ingenuity to find what is not there.

Indeed, the conception of Judaism as an organized body of doctrine, as in the sentence, *Judaism teaches*, or *Judaism says*, derives from an age in which people further had determined that Judaism belonged to the category of *religion*, and, of still more definitive importance, a religion was something that *teaches* or *says*. That is to say, Judaism is a religion, and a religion is (whatever else it is) a composition of beliefs. In Protestant theological terms, one is saved by faith. But the very components of that sentence, *one* -- individual, not the people or holy nation, *saved* -- personally, not in history, and saved, not sanctified, *faith* -- not *mitzvot* -- in fact prove incomprehensible in the categories constructed by Torah. In fact in the Torah one cannot make such a statement in that way. We have rather to speak as our subject of *Israel*, not one, to address not only individual life but all of historical time, so saved by itself does not suffice, further to invoke the verb, the category of sanctification, not only salvation, and to speak of *mitzvot*, not of faith alone. So the sentence serves for Protestant Christianity but not for the Torah. If, according to the Protestant theological category, I want to study a religion, I study what people believe. So of course

---

[4] That is why I called my prime textbook, *The Way of Torah*, and its companion-reader, *The Life of Torah*. But I see other ways to compose an introduction to Judaism and am now experimenting with one of them.

Judaism, for its part, will also teach things and lay down doctrines, even dogmas. But the category, faith, the work of constructing the system of thought of which the category is composed -- these do not serve for the study of the data we refer to, all in all, as Judaism.

Now, to revert to my grandmother, who in this setting serves as our native speaker, for her the counterpart of the statement, *Judaism teaches*, is, *the Torah requires*, and the predicate of such a sentence would be not, *...that God is one*, but, *...that you say a blessing before eating bread. Judaism* encompasses, classifies and organizes, *doctrines*: the faith, which, by the way, an individual adopts and professes. *Torah* teaches what we, God's holy people, are and must do. The one speaks of intellectual matters and beliefs, the latter, social actions and deeds of public consequence -- including, by the way, affirming such doctrines as God's unity, the resurrection of the dead and the coming of the Messiah, the revelation of the Torah at Sinai, and on and on: we can rival the Protestants in heroic deeds of faith.. So it is true, the faith demands deeds, and deeds presuppose faith. But, categorically, the emphasis is what it is: *Torah* on on God's revelation, the *canon*, to Israel and its social way of life, *Judaism* on a system of *belief*. That is a significant difference between the two categories, which, as I said, serve a single purpose, namely, to state the thing as a whole.

Equally true, one would (speaking systemically) also *study Torah*. But what one studied was not an intellectual system of theology or philosophy, rather a document of revealed Scripture and law. That is not to suggest that my grandmother did not believe that God is one, or that the philosophers who taught that Judaism teaches ethical monotheism did not concur that, on that account, one has to say a blessing before eating bread. But the categories are different, and, in consequence, so too the composites of knowledge. A book *on* Judaism explains the doctrines, the theology or philosophy, of Judaism. A book *of* the holy Torah expounds God's will as revealed in "the one whole Torah of Moses, our rabbi," as sages teach and embody God's will. I cannot imagine two more different books, and the reason is that they represent totally different categories of intelligible discourse and of knowledge. Proof, of course, is that the latter books are literally unreadable. They form part of a genuinely oral exercise, to be cited sentence by sentence and expounded in the setting of other sentences, from other books, the whole made cogent by the speaker. That process of homogenization is how *Torah* works as a generative category. It obscures other lines of structure and order. True, the two distinct categories come to bear upon the same body of data, the same holy books. But the consequent compositions -- selections of facts, ordering of facts, analyses of facts, statements of conclusion and interpretation and above all, modes of public discourse, meaning who says what to whom -- bear no relationship to one another, none whatsoever. Indeed, the compositions more likely than not do not even adduce the same facts, or even refer to them.

Why, in the study of ancient Judaism, do I find it necessary to pursue the rather abstract question of category-formation? The reason is that the issue of category-formation dictates the character of learning, and that is why I regard the matter as urgent. For until we have explained the answers to three questions, we pursue unexamined careers of hunting and gathering information for a purpose we cannot specify, sorting out data the cogency of which we cannot explain. What question does the analysis of category-formation answer? It is what we want to know, how we propose to find out, and why, to begin with, we ask.

Nothing in learning derives from nature, that is, the nature of the data. All things come from nurture and therefore culture, that is, the social exercise of learning. Each of the categories we invoke to impart meaning and order to our minds comes from somewhere. Categories so deeply mark our minds that they appear to us to be self-evident. But, as I have shown, each category finds self-evidence in its larger social context, therefore forms a construct, not a given, ultimately expressing an aspect of culture, political or economic expediency, or even consciousness and conscience -- what our Gallic masters call *interiority* -- as I shall explain presently.

II
The Social Construction of Categories

The premise of this book demands explicit statement at the outset. It is that categories take form in the context not of the unconstrained mind but of the social intellect: the imagination formed, made plausible, by society, culture, politics -- that is to say, context and circumstance. What we want to know society tells us we should find out. How we shall find out what we want to know culture explains. And beyond the two lies the social compact that imparts sense and acceptance to the facts we think we know and to the categories that legislate the rules of comprehension and collective understanding. These are common sense and self-evidence. They in the end form the criteria for description. Description lends order and meaning to discrete pieces and bits of information, so forming the beginning of comprehension, of knowledge. So what we want to know, that is, the categories of knowledge, and how we find it out, namely, through selecting appropriate data and analyzing them, come to us as the gifts and the givens of our social world. Our context, provides the technology of finding things out, identifying sources we want to study and determining how to read them, also specifying sources we ignore and explaining why they contain only gibberish. All these, when brought to the surface and examined, testify to the formation of the categories of our minds, the structure and construction of all knowledge. So category-formation forms the critical component of consciousness and defines the structure of understanding.

To give a simple example of the centrality of category-formation in the definition of how we shall understand social reality, I point to a case far away from the recognition of *Judaism* as a category, *Midrash* as its method,

Messianism as its uniform teleology. Rather, I refer to the recognition of *the* Maori as a social entity and -- more to the point -- organizing category of learning. In turning to far-off New Zealand, I want to know why that remote society falls into two parts, Maori and Pakeha (European), and, more especially, who first discovered that the Maori are Maori and why the discovery mattered. To frame the question simply: Did the Maori know they were Maori, and, if not, who told them? (The parallel? Did my grandmother know that the Torah was Judaism, and if not, why did her grandson have to find out?) The answer to that question follows:

> ...in attempting to describe *the* Maori and his culture, we are creating a stereotype that did not exist; for there was no one typical Maori but many Maoris; no one Maori culture but regional and tribal varieties of culture. Moreover, most observers were expert in the culture of only one or two areas, though they often passed off that information as representative of the Maori people as a whole. Even the name, Maori, is an abstraction, created in the nineteenth century. Cook called them Indians, though the name New Zealanders was soon applied. Maori (ordinary) was first recorded about 1800 as an adjective in the phrase *tangata maori,* an ordinary person, as contrasted with *tangata tupua,* a supernatural being, as the Europeans were first thought to be. By the 1830s Maori was being used occasionally as a proper noun, but it did not come into general use as such until about the 1860s. Since then it has been used retrospectively to describe the early inhabitants....5

In fact when the Europeans came, New Zealand consisted of two dozen different groups (social entities), at war among themselves, unaware that, as a whole, they formed a distinct society or nation or culture-group.

All they knew they had in common was that they lived on the same islands. That is to say, they shared the same planet, just as much as we share the same planet with Ethiopians or Peruvians, without regarding ourselves as part of a single entity (short of the human race, and that category bears slight consequence, when we dismiss sentimentality). Were explorers from a distant galaxy to come and call us all "the weirdos," the sense -- the self-evident appropriateness of the name -- would strike us as no different from the self-evident appropriateness of the name Maori, when applied to the twenty-four perpetually warring groups ("nations"? "tribes"?) of the North and South Islands. Someone from the moon might as well have appeared on the Somme in 1916 and announced that the French and the Germans formed one indivisible nation. Such a statement, in that circumstance, would not likely have enjoyed universal self-evidence. Whatever the diverse Maori called themselves, they saw differences where outsiders saw sameness, and, in consequence, they fought unceasing wars, living out their lives in stockades. So, descriptively speaking,

---

5 M. P. K. Sorrenson, *Maori Origins and Migrations* (Auckland, 1979: Auckland University Press and Oxford University Press), pp. 58-59.

the generative category, Maori, derived from elsewhere. To them it was not only not self-evident, it made no sense at all.

But under other circumstances, at a different time, and for a fresh purpose, the categorical self-evidence of *Maori* struck the Maori quite forcefully. So *Maori* became a self-evident category -- but not because of the character of the data to which the category applied. In fact the category proved contingent on circumstance: politics and interest, things not of the mind at all. So much for context and self-evidence! As Sorrenson says, *maori* meant ordinary, that is, the normal, *us*, as against the extraordinary, *them*, the supernaturals. But that is not what the word means now. Then it was a mode of organizing unfamiliar experience by distinguishing natural from supernatural data. Now it serves as a political category, classifying for racial purposes a diverse and mixed population. So do categories form and reform, now supernatural, now political,, now economic, in response to changing circumstance. When the New Zealand government today asks incoming travelers whether they are Maori, it does not mean to raise a theological question. And the question the government does address travelers remains one of classification. But the category has shifted, *and therefore also the facts.*

III

The Circumstantial Character of Categories
and of their Formation

Knowing consists in more than merely following the intellectual equivalent of the rules of syntax for language. Knowing always rests on selection among the things that are there to be known, as everyone knows. We may choose to ignore, as the Australian aborigines did when the Europeans came, or we may choose to recognize and take charge, like the Maori in New Zealand, who carefully constructed a myth to account for their ownership of the land and much else:

> ...Maoris had their own purposes to serve in reciting and recording oral traditions, myths, and legends. Above all there was the vital question of establishing titles to land, since genealogies showing descent from Maui and the commander of the ancestral canoe from Hawaiki could be used to establish a charter to land....Far from dying out as the Europeans expected, Maori traditions, myths, and legends, including those elaborated in the nineteenth century, have continued as a vital part of what is still very much an oral culture[6]

The Maori created categories in response to circumstance, and the categories then dictated the kinds of information they would collect or invent, as circumstance

---

[6] Sorrenson, pp. 84-5.

required. Indeed, I wonder whether the pre-historic, traditional tale, first told to be sure in the later nineteenth century, of the primeval or prehistoric migration by great canoe may in time turn out to be a restatement, with exquisite irony, of the (by-then-well-known) fact of the First Fleet, bringing the original settlers to Australia. But that is not our problem.

Understanding the categories that dictate what we want to know and how we shall find it out defines our problem. Yet, as is clear, I find much to learn in a field so alien, so distant, to the one at hand. For where on the face of the earth can we go further from the Near East and Europe, and what age can we locate, beyond our own, more remote from that of the Jews of late antiquity, in the first through the seventh centuries, than nineteenth century New Zealand. And how astonishing then is it to know, as Sorrenson says:

> ...the ethnographers nearly always found in Maori culture what they expected to find; their expectations were kindled by the prevailing anthropological theories of their day. In this respect the ethnographic record on the Maori is a fairly faithful reproduction of changing fashions in anthropology...Descriptions which purported to be of the Maori as he was at the time of Cook were often considerably influenced by the condition of contemporary Maoris.[7]

What conclusion do I draw from this observation? It is that theologically-motivated anachronism flourishes, not only in the study of the history of the Jews and Judaism in antiquity, but also in anthropology. In fact *everything* we know, we know because, to begin with, we require knowledge of one sort, rather than some other. And our context, that is to say, our circumstance in society and among the cultural groups of our own country, in our country among the countries of our region, and on upward, tells us what we need to know and why. In the study of social groups, for example, before recording facts, we know that the facts concern the social group at hand, and not some other. So we start with a definition of traits that distinguish a social group. The consequence is simple. If you have those traits, you are in the group, and if you do not, you are not in the group. I know the traits before I know the group that is defined by them, so to speak. That is why, as Sorrenson says, observers see what they anticipate seeing, and their expectations come from what they have already seen: the categories established in their minds.

The history of knowledge monotonously reminds us that people see what they expect to see, rarely noticing merely everything there is to see. In Sydney, I was told, when the ships of Captain Cook's fleet appeared at Botany Bay, the aborigines, farming on the shore, simply did not see them at all: they just did not *see* them. Not expecting such a sight, their eyes -- so people report -- perceived nothing at all. Whether or not the story is true, I cannot say. But it

---

[7]   Sorrenson, p. 58.

does conform to the rule that we see what we expect to see. In broader terms, we perceive through analogies, think in metaphors, interpret and understand the unknown in terms of the known, -- all this because there is no alternative.

Let me conclude with a simple example of these facts of learning and life. Describing the formation of knowledge about the Maori peoples of New Zealand, Sorrenson[8] further states:

> For most European observers were not content to record what they heard and saw; they had to interpret their information and above all to answer intriguing questions about the ultimate origin of the Maori and their coming to New Zealand....Europeans' answers to these questions and interpretations of Maori culture were profoundly influenced by the prevailing philosophies of man and the latest scientific techniques....The idea that mankind had diffused from a single point, usually in the Middle East or India, offered a starting point for interpretation. Comparative techniques in physical anthropology, culture, philology, and myths and legends offered means of proving ancient racial connections and of tracing the footsteps of primitive men, including the migrations of Polynesians. Darwinism offered a way of stretching the existing chronologies....These is no need to expand further on the absurdities of the Semitic or Aryan Maori theses -- both were attempts to apply the conventional wisdom of the day to the problem of the origin of the Polynesians....But it is worth pausing briefly to ask why the Maori was so favorably regarded: to be considered a Semite, when most other colored people were designated as Hamites; and, in the later nineteenth century, to be awarded the ultimate accolade of an Aryan ancestry like that of the Anglo-Saxon colonists? ....This was part of the wider ideal of an embryonic New Zealand nationalism. Nations are based on historical myths and New Zealand by the late nineteenth century was in the process of inventing hers.

So at the foundations of the category, *the Maori,* we uncover the demonic trinity, diffusionism, racism, and Social Darwinism! But as to the generative cause of the formation of that category, we uncover something considerably more within our range of understanding: the need of a new society, coming into existence out of the sherds and remnants of an older set of societies, to explain itself and its future[9]. And so too when it comes to "Judaism," "Midrash," and "The Messianic Doctrine of Judaism." What counterparts to such discredited ideas as diffusionism, Social Darwinism, or racism lie in the deep archaeology of these categories, of course, we cannot say. I see none. Nor do we know the

---

8   Sorrenson, p.82.

9   The invention of the Maori formed into a single category all of the (to themselves diverse) populations extant on the islands at the beginning of European settlement.   Today, I have the impression, the Maori assist the European-descended New Zealanders to accept their situation at the end of the earth and to let go of the long cord that binds them to "home," that is, "England."

human circumstances that made Jews look for a Judaism when they wanted to speak of the whole, all at once and all together, of their system.[10] But, to conclude, *Judaism* surely rests on a distinctive view of what we study when we study religion, and *Messianism* depends on the notion of a Judaism, and *Midrash* on yet another closely-dependent idea of continuity, which is that *Judaism* and *Christianity* (another hopeless category, but not our problem) meet in the interpretation of Scripture.[11]

IV

How Categories Take Shape: An Inductive Approach

A study of the history of category formation in the study of ancient Judaism carries us not into the first six centuries of the Common Era (A.D.) and off to the Land of Israel ("Palestine"), but to nineteenth and twentieth century Europe and America. There we should expect to find out where and why people determined that *Judaism* constituted a principal category for identifying information, organizing it, and lending it proportion, sense, meaning and even significance. Then too they reached the conclusion that *Midrash* formed the method, and *Messianism*, the teleological doctrine, of that same *Judaism*. These three categories therefore dictate the rules of description, determine the issues for analysis, and govern the hermeneutical alternatives explored in the interpretation of data. None is teased out of the data it is meant to categorize. All come from without -- some from far away indeed. An account of modern and contemporary consciousness among Jews would certainly tell us much about the formation of these categories, as expressions of what proved self-evident in the unfolding consciousness of the social group at hand.

---

[10] In his classic work, *The Uprooted*, Oscar Handlin argues that it was in America that the diverse immigrant groups discovered their shared nationality, e.g., as Italians. In Italy, if you asked, what are you and where do you come from, the answer would come as: from a village, such-and-so, in the province of X. In America, the *you* became Italian. So too the Jews of Eastern Europe described themselves by reference to village, near town, in province X. I never knew the name of my grandmother's village, all the more so that of the first Jacob Neusner, nor the name of their family, only, "near Koretz," in the "government of White Russia/Vohlynia. Jewish? Of course, so what? That did not count as a point of differentiation, therefore of category-formation. In America the immigrants gained that other identification, Jews as a group, Italians as a group. More to the point, the category made a difference. The self-consciousness that forces definition intellectually also expresses the power of homogenization working on internal points of distinction and differentiation within the social group. Wilfred C. Smith correctly has taught us that it is the outsider who names a religion, e.g., Hinduism. And, I would add, it is the experience of being the outsider that in the perception of the participant names the group.

[11] I shall spell this out in the relevant chapter. It is an explicit statement of Vermes that I have in mind.

My purpose here, however, is not to explore the history of how Jews and outsiders formed the category *Judaism* and so identified data they determined would form *Judaism*. What I wish to pose is a different question. It is an inquiry intimate to, generated by, the data I study, which is to say, the documents produced in late antiquity and from then to now preserved by Jews as God's revelation to Israel.

Specifically, I am trying to learn how to form appropriate categories for the description of *those* data, for the analysis of *those* data, and for the interpretation of *those* data. So my exercise in the study of category-formation begins not in abstract and philosophical reflection on nineteenth and twentieth century philosophy but in a particular body of the (to me) givens: the writings of the ancient sages, there alone. My study of category-formation therefore appeals to a particular authority: data already identified. It is inductive in a peculiar and curious way: I already know the limns and limits of my category,[12] and now I wish to find out what further categories have applied and whether they fit. My category is the canon of writings universally regarded by Jews from antiquity to the present day as Torah. My question is whether any other category than Torah applies. My answer is that none does. Specifically, the categories of *Judaism*, *Midrash*, and *Messianism* violate the limns and borders of the one category that forms from within the data and not outside of it, Those other categories, I shall try to show, therefore do not apply. That, sum and substance, is the argument of this book: the sole useful categories for the analysis of the Torah derive from the Torah.

---

12 In Chapter Four I confront the circularity of the present statement and show how to emerge from it.

Chapter One

Description:
The Category "Judaism"

The category, *Judaism*, unifies facts of belief into a system, a philosophy. *Judaism* tells us what we want to know, which is, statements of conviction open to intellectual analysis. *Judaism* tells us how to find out what we want to know, which is, in books of a certain authority, read as a harmonious testimony, and *Judaism* tells us how to find it out, which is, by reading those books and extracting from them the bits and pieces of information that serve our purpose. We then impart sense, meaning, proportion, and order to the data we find in the holy books: we create Judaism (now no longer a category, but a thing), or, rather, *a* Judaism, that is, a species of the genus *Judaism*, a system of thought derived from questions urgent to Jews of a certain order at a given moment, in a given place and time, and for a given circumstance. So the category *Judaism* in directing us to data of one sort rather than another proves contingent and dependent upon context.

How do we know it? Because, as I said in my homely story about my *bubbee*, if we examine the writings of Polish and Russian and German Jews in the eighteenth century, we look in vain for books with the word *Judaism* in their title, but if we examine the writings of Jews in the same parts of the world in the late nineteenth century, we find shelves of books that utilize in their title the word *Judaism*. So, as a postulate (not under investigation here) we may propose that Judaism is a construct, the invention of nineteenth century Jews, in particular, philosophical rabbis. But why, at that place and in that time, rabbis should turn into philosophers -- that too requires attention, in the study of the history of categories and their formation in -- *Judaism*.

I

The Protestant Origin of the Category, "Judaism"
Religion as Mainly a Matter of Faith:
Conscience versus Culture

The prevailing attitude of mind identifies religion with belief, to the near-exclusion of behavior, and in the hands of its academic scholars religion tends to identify itself with faith, so religion is understood as a personal state of mind or an individual's attitude. When we study religion, the present picture suggests, we ask about not society but self, not about culture and community but about conscience and character. It must follow that the category, Judaism, for the study of Judaism forms the counterpart to the category, Religion, for the study of religion. The categories are homologous, the one serving to identify data in general, the other, data in the Judaic context. So when we treat religion as a matter of conviction and conscience, hence of belief and not of culture, we adopt a definition of religion from a group that so defines religion, and we then make use of that definition in the formation of our categories for the study of ancient Judaism. When we study religion, we tend, in the aggregate, to speak of individuals and not of groups: faith and its substance, not societies and their systems of behavior and belief. Beyond faith, the category religion then encompasses the things that faith represents: faith reified, hence, religion.

Let me give as example of what I mean the observations by William Scott Green about the definition of Judaism operative in the mind of E. P. Sanders when Sanders describes rabbinic writings. In a debate with Sanders I had complained that his categories seem to me improperly formed, since the rabbinic texts do not conform to the taxonomy Sanders utilizes. They in other words are not talking about the things Sanders wants them to discuss. Sanders, Green says, "reads rabbinic texts by peering through them for the ideas (presumably ones Jews or rabbis believed) that lie beneath them. He thus ignores what the texts themselves actually talk about, the materials that attracted the attention and interest of the writers."[1] Sanders, in Green's judgment, introduces a distinct premise:

> For Sanders, the religion of Mishnah lies unspoken beneath its surface; for Neusner it is manifest in Mishnah's own language and preoccupations.[2]

Generalizing on this case, Green further comments in more general terms as follows:

> The basic attitude of mind characteristic of the study of religion holds that religion is certainly in your soul, likely in your heart, perhaps in your mind, but never in your body. That attitude encourages us to construe religion cerebrally and individually, to think in terms of beliefs and the believer, rather than in terms of behavior and community. The lens provided by this prejudice draws our attention to the intense and obsessive belief called "faith," so religion is understood as a state of mind, the object of intellectual or emotional commitment, the result of decisions to believe or to have faith. According to this model, people have religion but they do not do their religion. Thus we tend to devalue

---

[1] Personal letter, January 17, 1985.

[2] William Scott Green in his Introduction, *Approaches to Ancient Judaism* (Chicago, 1980: Scholars Press for Brown Judaic Studies) II, p. xxi.

behavior and performance, to make it epiphenomenal and of course to emphasize thinking and reflecting, the practice of theology, as a primary activity of religious people....The famous slogan that "ritual recapitulates myth" follows this model by assigning priority to the story and to peoples' believing the story, and makes behavior simply an imitation, an aping, a mere acting out.[3]

Now as we reflect on Green's observations, we of course recognize what is at stake. It is the definition of religion, or, rather, what matters in or about religion, emerging from Protestant theology and Protestant religious experience.

For when we lay heavy emphasis on faith to the exclusion of works, on the individual to rather than on society, conscience instead of culture, when we treat behavior and performance by groups as less important and thinking, reflecting, theology and belief as more important, we simply adopt as normative for academic scholarship convictions critical to the Protestant Reformation. Judaism and the historical, classical forms of Christianity, Roman Catholic and Orthodox, place emphasis at least equally on religion as a matter of works and not faith alone, behavior and community as well as belief and conscience. Religion is something that people do, and they do it together. Religion is not something people merely have, as individuals. So religion is something one may study, since religion generates matters of knowledge, not merely feeling and private opinion. Since the entire civilization of the West, from the fourth century onward, has carried forward the convictions of Christianity, not about the individual alone but about politics and culture, we may hardly find surprising the Roman Catholic and Orthodox Christian conviction that religion flourishes not alone in heart and mind, but in eternal social forms: the Church, in former times, the state as well. But for the social and cultural dimensions of religion, the present academic sciences of religion find little space.

Perhaps in the study of Judaism we place too much emphasis on society and behavior, performance and public action. We may ask too intensively about the relationship between the historical, including political, circumstance of a religious system and the statements of that system. In doing so, we may have carried too far the program of Max Weber in his investigation of the role of religion in economic and other modes of social behavior. But ours, if it is an excess, is idiosyncratic. The excess of others carries them deep into the definitions and convictions of the Protestant sector of Christianity. And, if truth be told, it is the Lutheran sector of Protestant Christianity that has taught us about the introspective conscience of the West, so we may hardly find astonishing the remarkable congruence between the academic study of religion in Germany and Lutheran conviction about what matters in religion. In fact, the academic study of religion derives its deepest convictions from theology, not from descriptive modes of learning Green phrases matters in this way:

---
[3] Personal letter, January 17, 1985.

The Protestant prejudice encourages us not to listen to what people actually say and not to watch what they actually do, but to suppose that these tractables are mere reflections of some underlying belief that is the ultimate grounding of the religious life. We need to reshape our collective curiosity and transcend the boundaries of this intellectual prejudice to acquire a fuller picture of the richness of the religious as they are lived, acted, and performed -- that is, to understand religions as we find them.[4]

Now I hasten to add, we have no reason to find surprising the dominance of Protestant attitudes toward religion. After all, the academic study of religion in America originated among Protestant scholars of religion. Adopting the categories as framed in that context hardly presents surprises.

That context, moreover, proves benevolent and inviting. The openness to diversity, the interest in the other, the capacity to pursue an other-than-narrowly-theological program -- these constitute the glories of the academic study of religion in America. And they are the gifts of Protestant scholars of religion. I should argue, moreover, that only Protestants could have so shaped the field -- Protestants of a particular order, to be sure. For they are the ones who took seriously and responded to the program of the Enlightenment, with its interest in a critical examination of religion. To be sure, for their own reasons, they affirmed the Enlightenment's view of religion as something personal and idiosyncratic, rather than public and social, so, for their own reasons, the Protestant founders of the study of religion found slight difficulty with the study of religion as belief, rather than behavior. True, religion then -- for both the Protestant framers of the field and the secular continuators of the Enlightenment -- is something one thinks or feels, not something about which one acquires knowledge.

Still, they -- heirs to the Enlightenment, founders and framers of the concept of religion as the generative category at hand -- are the ones who saw the study of religion as a generalizing science. No one else did, and few today try to generalize at all. The Protestants are the ones who asked not only about religions about also about religion. They are the ones who invited to give testimony not only religions they understood but also the ones they did not understand. They therefore founded the academic study of religion in this country and not the Jewish or Roman Catholic scholars. So it is not inappropriate to recognize their definitive role in the category-formation at hand.

Our intense interest in faith instead of religion as a social fact and a cultural determinant derives from our origins in Protestant theology, as that theology took shape at a particular moment in the history of American Protestant thought, on the one side, and American culture, on the other. I refer, of course, to the simple fact that our new, young field traces its origins to the immediate

---

[4]   Personal letter, January 17, 1985.

years after World War II, when America entered a position of world consequence. Then we had to pay attention to the "other," in all of the infinite diversity of humanity, in ways in which, before that time, we as a nation did not. The Protestant founders of the academic study of religion, the creators of the departments of religious studies we now find exemplary made a formidable contribution to the nation's capacity to confront the other and to sort out difference. In contributing the category, Judaism, to the academic study of religion, they cannot be faulted. But the category cannot serve any longer. The study of religion has now outgrown its Protestant origins. And the study of *Judaism* has consequently to compose categories appropriate to its data -- that is, generated out of the encounter with its data and yet serves to make possible statements intelligible beyond those data.

II
Alternative Categories:
From "Judaism" to "A Judaism"

The process of category-formation at a given time and place represents a response to circumstance and context. So we learn wherever we turn, from home in post-World War II America to far-away New Zealand to near-at-hand Germany, where, so to speak, in the turn of this century our minds were born.[5] For category-formation by definition constitutes a social act, working as it does to link one mind to the next, to provide a common setting for sense to serve society. Categories by definition take place in public. They help groups of people to draw together and to select facts and form them into intelligible patterns. Since categories serve as social modes of classification and organization of knowledge, they by definition must constitute political judgments of one kind or another.

For example, the category Judaism serves to join diverse systems and of belief and ways of life into a single encompassing system, Judaism, as in the sentence, "Many Judaisms teach....". Now that sentence, outside of the pages of the book, will prove unintelligible. But if we were to frame the sentence, "Many versions of Judaism teach....," then Reform Judaic theologians will find the statement in accord with their rules of thought and speech, and, as I said, the sentence, "Judaism teaches....," will prove sensible to all Judaic theologians. If, moreover, I were to offer the statement, "Many Judaisms form a single Judaism," which is a mere variation on the foregoing, historians of religion, but they alone, would understand. So let us explore the usage, *a Judaism*, in place of Judaism.[6] A Judaism comprises a world view and a way of life that together

---

[5] May we permit ourselves to imagine that, a hundred years from now, someone might write such a sentence about America? But why not? And where else?

[6] Not italicized, therefore not treated as a category.

come to expression in the social world of a group of Jews. "Judaisms" therefore constitute several such ways of life and world views brought to realization among communities of Jews. Why Judaisms, not Judaism?

In ancient times, as in every age of the histories of Jews, diverse groups of Jews defined for themselves distinctive systems: ways of life and world views addressed to a distinctive social group. We know one system from the other by reference to diverse indicators. To take one critical emblem, we refer to the generative symbol of a system, a Judaism. Were the symbol the same among all groups of Jews, we should have ample reason to imagine that all Judaisms form one Judaism.[7] But the generative symbols of distinct systems scarcely prove identical. To take one obvious example, the generative symbol of the Essene community at Qumran was not the same as that of the rabbinical community of, let us say, Pumbedita. The former can have employed a table, to symbolize the holy meal, or the Zodiac, to speak of the correspondence of heaven and earth, or even the Torah. But the latter -- by definition -- can have resorted only to a Torah-scroll. The former can have constructed the room in which it conducted its prayers (if it had such a special room) so that the visual focus lay at a number of places, but the latter can have designed a synagogue only so as to place the Torah-scroll at the visual center of matters. Again, if we look at the visual directions of the West wall of the synagogue at Dura-Europos, we find the visual focus on the Temple in Jerusalem -- hence the western wall. But, on that wall the eye focuses on the holy men of Israel, Moses, Aaron, and others, and through them on the salvific history of Israel.[8] True, the Torah-niche stood at the center. But it was surrounded by an explicit statement of what the Torah represented, what mattered in it: the repertoire of verses or stories that counted. In appealing to visual symbols, I mean to make a simple point. Different groups resorted to different symbols for the expression of the whole, so

---

[7] *From*, not *derive from*. The claim that the systems differ but all derive from the same source, therefore constitute really the same system, Judaism, evades the question. It presupposes that Scripture comes first, commencing a linear history of Judaism. But Scripture always defines the range of choices, and each group makes its own choices, and these choices differ from those of other groups. One group talks about one set of verses and imputes its meanings to them, and another group talks about a different set of verses and imputes its meanings to them, and it is rare for one group to talk about the same set of verses as another and to differ about the meaning of those verses, and rarer still for two groups to agree on the meanings, in detail, of the same group of verses -- and to regard the agreement as significant. So we need not be detained by the silly conception that all Judaisms come from one Judaism or find underlying unity in one Judaism. All Judaisms come from the groups that make them, and the groups that make them each make their own distinctive statement, their Judaism. The fact that all refer to the same source of proof-texts is more than adventitious, to be sure, since it permits us to speak of Judaisms.

[8] The compositors of Genesis Rabbah read Scripture in precisely the same way, looking for and finding the identical themes.

they drew upon different proof-texts of Scripture, and they therefore brought to expression wholes -- systems -- that were different from one another. Among three possible relationships, to which, in a moment, we shall return, namely, autonomy, connectedness, and continuity, they stood, in relationship to one another, at best in the second, but, more likely, in the first.

As I said, a Judaism therefore constitutes the world view and the way of life that characterize the distinctive system by which a social group of Jews sorts out its affairs. True, these several systems produced by different groups of Jews assuredly do exhibit traits in common. For example, they universally appeal to the same Hebrew Scriptures. But in fact points in common underline the systems' essential diversity. For if we ask a group to specify those verses of Scripture that it finds critical and to explain their meaning, we rarely hear from one a repertoire of verses found equally central in the system of some other distinct group. Still less do the interpretations of verses of Scripture among the several groups coincide. It follows that, in the history of Judaism, we identify different Judaisms. Whether we deal with a long period of time, such as a millenium or a brief period of just a few centuries, the picture is the same.

What then of the linear conception of the history of Judaism? It seems to me to misstate the way things actually happened among Judaisms. How so? Judaisms flourished side by side. Or they took place in succession to one another. Or they came into being out of all relationship with one another. So some Judaisms took shape all by themselves, remaining autonomous. Other Judaisms related to one another through connections of shared doctrine or practice that joined one Judaism to the next. And still other Judaisms turn out, upon inspection, to have formed a continuity and to have stood sequence with one another, so that the frontier between one and the next proves difficult to delineate.

So far I have written as though people in general used such words as "a Judaism."[9] But this very mode of thought is fresh. So let me back up and deal with the terms and categories people do know. How do people ordinarily define categories in sorting out Judaic data? What modes of thought dictate the questions they ask and methods of answering them? There is one category, "Judaism," and a single mode of thought, collecting and arranging Judaic data to testify to doctrines and practices of that Judaism, which people call Orthodox. They further regard this Judaism as the outcome of a linear and one-dimensional

---

[9] Likewise, I write as if people understood that the Messiah-theme in diverse Judaisms either may take an important systemic position or may contribute little to the system at hand. In Chapter Three I treat the diversity of messiah-materials, showing that they hardly constitute *the* doctrine of Messianism in *Judaism.*. My claim is that there are messiah-materials that circulate, some used here, some used there, but no basis for a book on *the* Messiah-doctrine in Judaism (unless, to begin with, we know that all data speak of a common Judaism). This is the burden of my *Messiah in Context* (Philadelphia, 1984: Fortress).

history, beginning, if not at Sinai (as the Orthodox maintain) then somewhere we can locate. Accordingly, people invoke the term "Judaism," meaning, "*the* Jewish religion*.*" They further employ the category of "Messianism," or "the Messianic doctrine in Judaism," as we shall note in Chapter Three. Hence we have books constructed upon the foundation of the species, "Judaism," within the genus, religion, Messianic.[10] Since the reader likely takes for granted that there really is only one Judaism, and that that one, official or normative or Torah-true "Judaism" teaches this and practices that, what has already been said must present some puzzles. First, how do we know one Judaism from some other? Second, on what basis do we claim to differentiate one system from some other. The two questions go together.

III

An Exercise in Category-Formation

My premise is what unites them. That simple premise holds that each piece of evidence demands inspection on its own. I cannot imagine a more self-evidently right approach to any problem of learning. We take each relevant item of information as it comes, working inductively from item to item, building a larger picture out of smaller components. That work of sifting and sorting of evidence characterizes all fields of Western learning. The analytical method has defined all learning from the beginning, in Greek science and philosophy, to our own day: observation, reflection. Curiosity reaches expression then in the questions, why? what if? and why not? But that mode of thought, based on observation and testing, scarcely characterizes the deductive system commonplace in the received and established methods of Judaic learning, a system that shamelessly invokes *a priori* facts of history and deductive categories of philosophy or theology, and that knows things before proof or without proof. So the present approach contradicts the established conviction.

That conviction, that all pieces of evidence deriving from Jews, whoever they were, wherever and whenever they lived, without regard to context and circumstance testify to one and the same Judaism, is represented as self-evident. It is not self-evident to me. So, like my grandmother, I pose problems to the people who hold the particular truth at hand to be self-evident. The truth is merely a proposal. That proposition remains to be demonstrated. What we cannot show we do not know. So here we propose to find out.

Why is it not obvious to me that the category, *Judaism*, defines our selection and use of evidence produced by Jews concerning their systems -- way

---

10   But in Chapter Three we turn matters on their head. We ask about the classification, or genus, Judaisms, and we invoke the Messiah-theme to help us differentiate one species of the genus, Judaisms, from another, thus, Judaisms and their messiahs. We accordingly move from one set of categories and modes of analysis to another.

of life and world view addressed to their social group? People familiar with the rich diversity of Christianity today and throughout the history of the Christian faith know the answer. To them it is not obvious that there is now, or even has been, one Christianity. They know that history has yielded, east and west, many Christianities -- united before the cross of Christ, but nowhere else. They will find routine the allegation that, just as history has yielded its diverse Christianities, in some ways autonomous, in some connected, in some ways continuous, so history testifies to more than one Judaism. Why does everyone understand that there is not now, and never was, a single Christianity (except, I hope, from God's perspective)? Because people consider the alternative. And that is a construct of total confusion, a harmony of opposites. Imagine the Christianity we should define and describe, were we to treat all evidence as uniform in the manner in which we treat the evidence about "Judaism." That would be a Christianity, to which Orthodox and heterodox, Arian and Athanasian, Greek and Russian, Armenian and Latin, Catholic and Gnostic, not to mention Protestant and Roman Catholic today, equally testify -- and all totally out of context. United in the cross of Christ? Indeed so -- but so what? For such a single Christianity unites around the cross, but divides on all else -- beginning, after all, with the cross itself.[11]

Then how about the Christianity of the first century? Do we not here, at least, deal with a single Christ? Few who have studied the problem would concur. The Gospels speak for diverse records of a single person. Each represents matters in a way distinctive to is authorship. All address points of disharmony in the nascent and tiny churches of the day. From the explanation of repeated stories and sayings settled by the theory of a Sermon on the Mount and a Sermon on the Plain (parallel to the harmonization of the two versions of the Ten Commandments, the one in Exodus, the other in Deuteronomy, by the theory that "remember" and "keep" were said at one and the same time), nearly all scholarship has taken a fond farewell. The last persuasive harmony of the Gospels found its original audience in the third century. For Christians it is routine therefore to read Matthew's Gospel as the statement of his school, its version of matters, and not as part of "the Gospels" single testimony to the one and uniform "life of Jesus." To speak of Mark's or John's or Matthew's viewpoint, the particular perspective of the author of Hebrews, not to mention the Christian systems of Aphrahat on east, Chrysostom in the center, or Augustine in the far West -- that is routine. No one proposes to force all evidence to testify to one Christianity.

Nothing presents a surprise, therefore, if we turn to the diverse and various texts of Judaism within a different premise from the one that holds, as a matter of hypothesis, the sources' deep and total harmony. The bits and pieces of evidence about "Judaism" in fact yield glimpses into diverse systems, various

---

[11] I refer to the diversity of Christologies that divide Christianities.

Judaisms. Each comes from its own setting and to begin with is to be described and analyzed in its original context, its time, its place, its circumstance. Anyone, for instance, who imagines that we can explain the art of the synagogue at Dura Europos or the commonplace use of the Zodiac in mosaic floors of synagogues in harmony with the prohibition of graven images and the Talmud's interpretation of that prohibition begins from premises other than those paramount in Western learning. For in the West we prefer to differentiate, through comparison and contrast, before we consider how (if at all) to harmonize; we analyze before we synthesize; we make discrete observations before we propose to explain. We test hypotheses before we reach conclusions. So the Judaism of Dura Europos or of the decorated synagogues an the Judaism represented in the pages of the writings of the ancient rabbis have to be described, each by itself and in its own terms. Only then are they to be compared. Whether or not, at the end, people will wish to harmonize the whole range of Judaisms into a single Judaism we do not now know, for the first two steps await us. The matter at hand derives not only from the established conceptions of the Western humanities and social sciences, so alien overall to the closed system of Judaic Studies. The evidence at hand itself demands the procedures of differentiation and inductive category-formation advocated in this book. Why so? Because, as I suggested at the outset, diverse groups of Jews in late antiquity produced varied kinds of evidence, some in art and symbol, some in writing; some in the writing of visions, some in the writing of laws.

If, therefore, we posit a single Judaism, what are we to make of the mass of confused evidence? Which group and which type of evidence shall we select for our description of "Judaism" (as distinct from a Judaism)? And how shall we know the Orthodox from the heretic? Any judgment that one group attests more authentically than some other what defined "Judaism" constitutes a theological (or, among Israeli secularists, national) and not a descriptive and analytical statement. That acutely contemporary judgment itself demands description, analysis, and interpretation in its own terms. Why? Because today it presents an important statement of the religious perspective of a Judaism. But it is not a fact about the whole of Judaism (in my language, all "Judaisms"), except among those who believe it, also, to constitute a dogma of Judaism. So if we propose to make sense of the data deriving from diverse Judaists (practitioners of a Judaism) in late antiquity, our first task requires analysis and differentiation. Only much later on shall we want to know what joins the parts into a single whole, if anything does. And still later, among believing Jews (among whom I count myself) may emerge the question of norm and truth,a s distinct from fact and description: which statement really constitutes revelation, that is, torah from Sinai? that question demands its answer in its setting, which self-evidently is not this one.

For we who study religion propose in the setting of the public (hence, not theological) inquiry into the nature of religion to describe, analyze, and interpret.

We think there are things to know about religion, not merely religious beliefs or feelings to record. Seeing religion as an object of knowledge, we try to analyze and compare, describe and interpret, as we do any other topic of social inquiry. The *we* is made up of learning people, atheists, Christians and Jews[12] alike, who respect the religions that have emerged from late antiquity to define the civilization of the West and of the world, the Christianities, the Judaisms (become the Judaism for much of its history). But we come to this study because we are children of the tradition of Western philosophy, that is, because we want to know how things came to be the way they are: What if? and why? and why not?

Having said who we are, I return to the question at hand. On what basis do we claim to differentiate data that describe one system, that is, one Judaism, from those that testify to another, and how shall we know one from another? To state the task of discovering a Judaism in the facts at hand, very simply, we work inductively. We take up each document[13] or artifact (whether in writing or in tactile form, whether in words or in symbols) and look at that piece of evidence, all by itself, entirely on its own terms.[14] We ask that piece of evidence a number of questions, thereby trying to classify it. What kind of evidence is at hand? Who is likely to have produced it? What is its primary context? Who then is apt to have received it, absorbed it, made use of it in some other, different or later context? These are the sorts of questions that open the way toward the description of the evidence, item by item. The answers to these questions tell us how to describe an autonomous piece of evidence, on the one side, and to relate one piece of evidence to some other, on the other.

Clearly, what I propose calls to mind the well-tried labor of natural history, with its careful examination of the specimens, leading to the recognition of a species, and of several species, leading to the definition of a genus. When the several genera reach full definition and, moreover, clearly participate in a common environment, we have come upon what some might call an ecosystem, and what, in the context of society, culture, and religion, we may call a system, or a religion, or, in the present setting, a Judaism. Now in the case at hand, we take up a diversity of sources produced by Jews in a single period of time and place. The time is late antiquity, mainly from ca. 200 B.C. to ca. A.D. 200. These authors lived in the territory we Jews call "the Land of Israel," and in later

---

[12] The academic study of religion, as distinct from the theological study of religions by believers, flourishes only among Christians, Jews, and atheists, and, mainly, among Protestant Christians. This point will become important shortly.

[13] In Chapter Four I argue that, for the study of the Judaism that took shape in late antiquity, we work within the documents of the canon of that Judaism as universally identified and recognized by representatives of that Judaism.

[14] As I said, in Chapter Four I confront the circularity the reader will perceive in that statement. I do claim to demonstrate a simple and entirely inductive principle of category-formation.

times others called Palestine. What we now propose to do is to read these diverse sources with a single analytical question in mind, as I explained.

But how does that reading yield the notion that we deal with "a Judaism"? And shall we claim that a book is a system, and does a document, by itself, testify to a religion? Asking the question underlines its absurdity. No one claims a book equals a system. A book testifies only to the system of which it is part. We know the book forms a detail of a system, a Judaism, when the evidence defining the provenience of the book tells us so, for example, it turns up in a library revered by a community, or it is preserved for centuries as an authoritative or "Torah-true" document. The delineation of the system of which a book or an idea forms a part begins in the detail constituted by the single document or the naked idea. So when we turn to a given document, we derive a detail that, we hope, will point us toward the whole system of which the document constitutes a component, that is to say, the larger system attested by this artifact. In that case, the category at hand derives from the canon of which the book forms a part. The book, the document, then defines a detail, and the canon of which it is part, the whole. True, God lives in the details. But how shall we call God up -- I mean, the system as a whole -- out of the details? And when we call, will anyone answer us and make an appearance? That question defines our task in the labor of category-formation before us.

Chapter Two

Analysis:
The Category "Midrash"

One of the criteria for the use of forming a category is that category's effect in facilitating analysis, hence, comparison and contrast. If a category effects distinctions within evidence, we wonder whether these distinctions divide matters up in such a way that one group of data permits comparison with another, equivalently defined group. Should we discover that we are comparing things that are not sufficiently alike to warrant comparison, we may learn that our original principle of category-formation was awry. If, on the other hand, our comparisons and contrasts prove illuminating, so that we compare comparables and therefore find distinctions among them, gaining perspective on the context and meaning of the whole, then the original principle of category-formation finds solid vindication.[1]

For a useful category tells us what to compare and how to effect the comparison. A useless one does not. The category, *Midrash*, is one that, within the present scheme of category-formation, ordinarily serves to effect comparison -- the field is called *Comparative Midrash* --, and on that account, we focus upon that category in our analysis of the received categories. But that is not the only reason, in our inquiry into the analytical power of the received system of categories, to turn to *Midrash* in particular.

The importance of the present category for the system represented by the category, *Judaism*, rests on a further fact. People who take for granted a linear development of a single Judaism also appeal to Scripture in justification of the postulate of that single Judaism. Why is this so? It is clear, in viewing this linear Judaism, that Judaism teaches things that Scripture does not say. When explaining how Scripture can yield notions not found in Scripture, they appeal to the category, *Midrash*, as the method of *Judaism* in linking Judaism's principles to Scripture. So *Midrash* forms a key-component in the larger intellectual structure represented by the category, *Judaism*.

To return to the point at which I started, I mean to make a single point. The faulty formation of the category at hand and its use for comparative purposes accounts for consequent, and enormous flaws in the way in which

---

[1] I recognize the circularity of the argument at its present stage.

Comparative Midrash presently undertakes description, analysis, and interpretation of differences in opinion on the meaning of the same verse of Scripture. Those differences, as we shall see, are what is catalogued and spelled out in *Comparative Midrash*. Hence, as I said, the results of the present system of category formation now come under assessment: do we work with categories that facilitate analysis through comparison and contrast? Or do the received categories obscure difference and promote harmonization, rather than analysis? To these questions we shall find our way.

I

Defining the Category *"Midrash"*

The word *midrash* means exegesis, and at issue is how we compare the work and results of exegesis of Scripture -- the Hebrew Bible or Old Testament -- produced by Judaic and Christian exegetes. This sort of comparative study engages the attention of scholars of the history of Judaism and of Christianity and the comparison of systems of Judaism and of Christianity to one another. A sizable literature compares materials in that classification of writing. That literature studies Judaic, sometimes also Christian, exegesis of the Old Testament and compares the results achieved by one group with those produced by another, either within Judaism or deriving from Christianity. So a subdivision of the study of the exegetical writings of the Hebrew Scriptures compares one *midrash* to another *midrash*. *Comparative midrash* then is an exercise in comparison. Therefore when we describe the methodological requirements of that type of comparison, we may learn some lessons useful for other types of comparison, e.g., of religion to religion.

What, exactly do we compare, when we compare one *midrash* to another *midrash* ? The first question before us is the meaning of the word *midrash*. *Midrash* stands for many things, but, in the main, the word is used in three ways.

First of all, *midrash* refers to the processes of scriptural exegesis carried on by diverse groups of Jews from the time of ancient Israel to nearly the present day. Thus people say, "He produced a *midrash* on the verse," meaning, "an exegesis." A more extreme usage produces, "Life is a *midrash* on Scripture," meaning that what happens in the everyday world imparts meaning or significance to biblical stories and admonitions. It is difficult to specify what the word *midrash* in Hebrew expresses that the word *exegesis* in English does not. It follows that quite how "exegesis" in English differs from *midrash* in Hebrew, or why, therefore, the Hebrew will serve better than the more familiar English, I do not know. Some imagine that *midrash* for Jewish exegetes generically differs from *exegesis* for non-Jewish ones. What characterizes all exegeses produced by Jews, but no exegeses produced by non-Jews, who presumably do not produce *midrashim* on verses but do produce exegeses of verses of the same Hebrew Scriptures, I cannot say. Accordingly, the first usage seems so general as to add up to nothing. That is to say, *midrash*, a foreign word, simply refers to the same thing -- the activity or process or intellectual pursuit -- as exegesis, an English word. The word *midrash* bears no more, or less, meaning than the word *exegesis*.

The other two usages will detain us considerably less, since they bear a precision lacking in the first. The word midrash further stands for [2] a compilation of scriptural exegeses, as in "that *midrash* deals with the book of Joshua." In that sentence, *midrash* refers to a compilation of exegeses, hence the statement means, "That compilation of exegeses deals with the book of Joshua." *Compilation* or composite in the present context clearly serves more accurately to convey meaning than *midrash*. I use both words in this book. The word *midrash*, finally, stands for [3] the written composition (e.g., a paragraph with a beginning, middle, and end, in which a completed thought is laid forth), resulting from the process of *midrash*. In this setting "*a midrash*" refers to a paragraph or a unit of exegetical exposition, in which a verse of the Hebrew Scriptures is subjected to some form of exegesis or other. In this usage one may say, "Let me now cite the *midrash*," meaning, a particular passage of exegesis, a paragraph or other completed whole unit of exegetical thought, a composition that provides an exegesis of a particular verse. I use the word composition in this sense.

Accordingly the word bears at least three distinct, if related, meanings. If someone says "the *midrash* says," he may refer to [1] a distinctive *process* of interpretation of a particular text, thus, the hermeneutic, [2] a particular compilation of the results of that process, thus, the composite of a set of exegeses, or [3] a concrete unit of the working of that process, of scriptural exegesis, thus the write-up of the process of interpretation as it applies to a single verse, the exegetical composition on a particular verse (or group of verses).

It follows that for clear speech the word *midrash*, standing by itself, bears no meaning. In place of the word *midrash*, I prefer to use three words:

[1] exegesis, for *midrash* in the sense of an exegesis (of indeterminate character) of a verse of Scripture;

[2] composite, or compilation of exegeses (or occasionally, compilation of *midrashim*), for *midrash* in the sense of a sustained and sizable set or sequence or group of exegeses or even for a whole book made up of exegeses of Scripture;

[3] and unit of discourse, unit of thought, whole or completed unit of thought, composition, or similar expressions, for *midrash* in the sense of a single paragraph or a single fully spelled out essay of exegesis of a given verse or group of verses. The diverse meanings attached to the word hardly suggest the category at hand serves with much precision to tell us what fits, or does not fit. But that hardly presents a considerable obstacle, since at the end I shall offer as my generative category so imprecise a word as *Torah*. By itself the word

neither validates nor disqualifies the category for which it stands. At issue? It is how the category, Midrash, today serves analytical work: comparison and contrast.

II

Comparative *Midrash*

The inquiry of *comparative midrash* today encompasses three distinct activities. People may mean that they wish to compare [1] processes or methods of exegesis of Scripture (e.g., hermeneutics), [2] compilations of exegeses of Scripture (but this is uncommon), or [3] specific exegeses of a given verse of Scripture with other exegeses of the same verse of Scripture (this being the most commonplace activity of the genre). Let me now clarify the inquiry into comparison and place the work on firmer epistemological and methodological foundations. For when colleagues reflect on what they are doing, they may well find reason to redefine and reorder their agenda of inquiry.

When we compare, we seek, first, perspective on the things compared. Second, we look for the rule that applies to the unfamiliar thing among the things compared. The unknown thing is like something else, therefore falls under the rule governing the known thing to which it is likened, or it is unlike something else, therefore falls under the opposite (or, at least, another) rule. We compare, third, so as to discover the context for interpreting the things compared. How so? Through comparison we uncover traits that are unique to one thing and therefore also those that are shared among the things compared.

In these three -- as well as in other -- ways the labor of comparison and contrast forms the foundation of all inquiry into otherwise discrete and unintelligible data. Without [1] perspective, [2] knowledge of the applicable rule, and [3] a conception of the context, we understand only the thing itself -- and therefore nothing at all. For what is unique by definition is beyond comprehension. The reason is that we understand what is not yet known by reference to metaphors supplied by the things already understood: their perspective, the pertinent rule governing them, the understanding of them gained in knowledge of their context. The work of comparison and contrast, classification and interpretation of discrete data, defines all rational inquiry. The sole alternative, the claim of *a priori* understanding of things incompletely known, requires no attention because it lies outside of rational inquiry, for we have no way of falsifying, therefore verifying, *a priori* allegations concerning knowledge.

So we come to "comparative *midrash*" in particular. What, precisely, do we compare when we compare *midrash[im]* ? The answer will derive from asking how properly to compare one thing with something else, in this case one *midrash* with another *midrash*. The reader will immediately wonder which of the three meanings I have found in the word *midrash* defines the question of this book.

Do I mean comparing [1] hermeneutics, one mode of exegesis of Scripture with some other, for example, comparing the methods of *midrash*/exegesis of Matthew with the methods of *midrash*/exegesis of the Essene writers of Qumran's library?

Do I mean [2] comparing redactional and formulary plans and theological programs, the definitive traits of one compilation of exegeses/*midrashim* with another such compilation, for example, Matthew Chapter Two with an equivalent composition of the Habakkuk commentary or with an equivalent passage of the Sifre to Numbers?

Or do I mean comparing [3] the substantive results -- treatment of a given verse of Scripture/*midrash* in one compilation of exegeses/*midrashim* with the treatment of that same verse or theme of Scripture/*midrash* in another compilation of exegeses/*midrashim*?

Since the phrase, "comparative *midrash*," has applied quite comfortably to all three types of comparison, the answer to my question cannot emerge from common usage. That is because, it seems to me self-evident, common usage is confused. Here I propose to clarify and purify that usage.

I do so by arguing that, to begin with -- but only to begin with -- the work of comparative *midrash*, should commence with classification [2], compilations, whole documents, and not classification [1] with modes of exegesis of Scripture occurring here, there, and everywhere, and also not with classification [3] discrete parts of documents . What should be compared at the outset is [2] whole to whole, document to document, and only later on [3] the constituent element of one document with the constituent element of another document, and last of all [1] the exegetical techniques, policies, or issues of one document with those of a second document.

Why begin with the entirety of [2] a composite of exegeses, rather than with [1] techniques or modes of exegesis, on the one side, or [3] the results of exegesis, on the other? The reason is simple. Comparison begins in the definition of things that are to be compared. That means we must know *that* things fall into a common genus, and only then shall we be able to ask *how* things are different from one another.

I maintain on the basis of logic that we first of all must determine the role of the context -- the document at hand -- in imparting to the materials contained within a document the document's framers' preferences in matters of both style and intellectual perspective or viewpoint. Only when we know the impact of the documentary context upon the materials in a document can we take up an individual item from that document and set it into comparison and contrast with an item drawn out of some other, also carefully delineated and defined, document. At the point at which we can define the traits distinctive to one documentary context we may ask about traits of an item that occur in other documentary contexts in which that item makes its appearance.

Why then must we first start with the definition of the documentary context, the whole of a compilation of exegeses? The documentary context stands first in line because it rests upon the firmest premise: it is what we know for sure. No speculation whatever leads us to the claim that [1] a given method of exegesis has yielded [3] a given exegetical comment on a verse of Scripture, the result of which is now in [2] this particular document. Since we know that wonderfully simple fact, what is found in which document, we can begin the work of describing the traits imparted by [2] that document to the [3] exegetical result of [1] the exegetical method at hand. Traits characteristic of [2] the documentary setting likewise emerge without a trace of speculation. If a document routinely frames matters in accord with one repertoire of formal conventions rather than some other, and if it arranges its formal repertoire of types of units of discourse in one way, rather than some other, we can easily identify those traits of the passage under study that derive from the documentary context.

Accordingly, we begin with the document because it presents the first solid fact. Everything else then takes a position relative to that fact. What then are some of the documentary facts? Here are some: this saying or story occurs here, bears these traits, is used for this larger redactional and programmatic purpose, makes this distinct point in its context (or no point at all). One may readily test these allegations and determine their facticity. These facts therefore define the initial context of interpretation. The facts deriving from the documentary setting define the context in which a given trait shared or not shared among the two discrete items to be compared.

In laying emphasis on the document as the correct first point of comparison, I exclude the candidacy for the appropriate point of departure for comparative studies of two others, namely, [1] modes of exegesis, hence, comparative hermeneutics, and [3] results of exegesis, hence, comparison of the exegesis of a verse in one document, deriving from one period and group of authorities, with the exegesis of that same verse in some other document, deriving from a completely different sort of authorities and a much earlier or much later period. No. 1 is uncommon, but No. 3 is the principal arena for *Comparative Midrash* today. In both cases I maintain that the context for comparison is improper, with the result that the work of comparison produces mere information, but no insight. Why do I maintain both grounds for comparison and contrast -- method, result, as against document -- lay infirm foundations?

Let me answer the question by raising a question. What do we *not* know if at the outset of comparing things we ignore what I regard as the first and fundamental issue, the plan and program of the document in which an item appears? If we ignore as unimportant the characteristic traits of the documentary location(s) of an exegesis of a verse of Scripture or of a story occurring in two ore more documents, or if we treat as trivial the traits characteristic of those locative points, we do not know the rule governing both items subject to comparison. We establish no context that imparts meaning to the work of comparison. Why not? Because we have no perspective on similarities and differences among the two or more things that are compared with one another. Similarities and differences may prove merely adventitious. But we shall never know. Points of likeness may constitute mere accidents of coincidence, e.g., of internal logic of the statement of the verse of Scripture at hand.

Let me offer a silly possibility of argument. If people in different places, times, or groups concur that a verse means one thing and not some other thing, it may be that that is because the meaning on which diverse groups concur is the only meaning the verse can yield. How do we know that that meaning, shared among diverse groups, is the only possible meaning? It is proved by the fact of broad concurrence among different groups (!). What is the upshot of this marvelously circular mode of reasoning? The claim that, because the items are alike -- say the same thing, for example, about the same verse -- therefore we know something we otherwise would not know about [1] hermeneutics, [2] documentary context, or [3] the history and meaning of the exegesis of the verse at hand, does not permit us to invoke processes of falsification or verification. Why not? Because, not knowing the *context* of likeness or difference, we also do not know the *meaning* of likeness or difference. That is why the definition of the context in which discrete data make their appearance demands attention first of all. But -- I repeat -- it is only first in sequence. *Comparative midrash* in sequence also will take up questions of [1] shared or different techniques and also [3] shared or different exegetical results in discrete settings. These two define further points of interest. But we must start at the largest and most general stage of description, the one resting on no speculation as to the facts, that is, therefore, the stage of establishing context: defining the genus prior to comparing the species.

Up to now we have enjoyed the results of comparison of [1] *techniques* of exegesis and [3] *results* of exegesis. These results derive from observations made wholly out of documentary context. But comparing what has not been shown comparable yields mere information, in the category of such a statement as this: apples are different from Australians. Out of context that information proves not merely trivial but mindless. How so? Apples and Australians are alike and may be compared and contrasted because they both begin with an A. Another point in common is that both apples and Australians thrive in parts of the great island-continent of Australia. Now anyone who has visited Sydney knows that in general Australians, living in the South Pacific sun, are ruddy. Everyone knows that all apples have stems. It furthermore is true that not all apples have rosy cheeks, for some are green or yellow, and no Australians have stems and grow on trees. But so what? That information leads us deep into a unending wonderland of odd information. Lacking all context, the generality of results of *comparative midrash* as presently practiced compares apples to Australians. That is to say, masses of information gained by comparing what may or may not prove consequential when compared or even comparable at all fills books lacking all program and inquiry. One can produce a great many such books without explaining explain what is at stake in any one of them. That explanation demands an answer to the question, what *else* do we know if we know the result of this inquiry of comparing A to A?

In other words we must be able to state what is at stake in observing that apples differ from Australians because Australians have ruddy cheeks and some apples are green, on the one hand, apples have stems and Australians do not, on the second hand, and both apples and Australians are known to thrive in Australia, on the third hand, and on and on. Inquiry must rest upon a point of interest, a hypothesis, a theory, a mode of validation and invalidation. We must know what we know -- which is to say, what *else* we know -- if we know the result at hand: this is like that, this is not like that.

Comparison and contrast therefore depend, in strict logic, upon prior identification of appropriate commonalities. The genus comes before the species. When we know that in consequential ways things are alike, we then can discover in what ways they are not alike. We further can derive further insight from the points in common and the differences as well. We cannot ask how things differ if we do not know that there is a basis for the question of comparison and contrast. And the point of distinction between one thing and another thing must be shown to make a difference.

If we do not ask the question concerning, in Jonathan Z. Smith's phrase, what difference a difference makes,[2] then we are comparing apples to Australians. Only when we can demonstrate that diverse objects fall into a single appropriate genus -- are all apples, for example, or are all Australians -- can we differentiate the species of the appropriately-defined genus, apple from apple, Australian from Australian. And that point of differentiation -- the distinction at hand -- must make a difference, must tell us something else about either apples or Australians. Knowing that apples and Australians have in common a point of origination on the same great continent tells us a point in common that yields no more useful insight than that both begin with the letter A. The distinctions we draw then also make no difference. We learn no "something else."

2.   Jonathan Z. Smith, "What a Difference a Difference Makes," in J. Neusner and E. S. Frerichs, eds., *"To See Ourselves as Others See Us." Christians, Jews, "Others" in Late Antiquity* (Atlanta, 1985: Scholars Press Studies in the Humanities), pp. 3-48.

III

Faulty Category Formation: Geza Vermes

Principal practitioner of *Comparative Midrash* in the senior generation,[3] Geza Vermes has provided in writing two expositions of his views of the enterprise. We review them in the order of their appearance. As before, I make comments on some main points. The first derives from Geza Vermes:[4]

> R. BLOCH investigates the biblical origins of the midrash in the post-exilic books of the Bible. She ascribes the birth of the midrashic genre to the progressive fixation of the text of Scripture during the Persian period, and suggests that its most characteristic examples appear in the Wisdom literature; but other examples are included in the exilic and post-exilic Prophets, and in Chronicles, the latter being a midrash on Samuel-Kings combined with the Priestly source of the Pentateuch (genealogies). The evolution of the midrash is followed within the "biblical milieu": The Apocrypha, (Ecclesiasticus, Wisdom of Solomon), Pseudepigrapha (Jubilees, Testaments of the Twelve Patriarchs), the Dead Sea Scrolls, the Septuagint, the choice of Qere (text to be read) to replace Ketib (written text), the Palestinian Targums, and finally the New Testament, where all the midrashic forms are presented.
>
> The wholly novel element in this synthesis is the systematic effort to situate the problem of the midrash within a proper historical perspective, not only as regards halakhah, but also haggadah. If all midrash, even haggadic, is an historical phenomenon whose origins are to be traced to post-exilic biblical times, the condition sine qua non for its understanding is to consider it within the setting of its evolution, to distinguish the stages of this evolution, and determine the causes of change. The whole significance of a midrashic theme cannot be understood without some knowledge of its history, and possibly of its pre-history. For example, the same interpretation of a scriptural story may be discovered in a mediaeval midrash, in the Talmud, in the Targum, in a Tannaitic collection, in JOSEPHUS, and -- let us say -- in Jubilees or Ecclesiasticus. This would mean that the fundamental exegesis is at least as old as the second century BC. The differences in its application at various periods may result from changes in aims, needs, or even doctrines; but such changes cannot be detected without knowing what exactly has been altered. To phrase it differently, the real significance of a Tannaitic haggadah can only be determined by comparing it with an interpretation of the same text by a pre-Tannaitic author and by an Amora.[5]

---

[3] In my *Comparative Midrash. The Plan and Program of Genesis Rabbah and Leviticus Rabbah* (Atlanta, 1986: Scholars Press for Brown Judaic Studies,) I present in the Appendix other practitioners of the same kind of comparison, specifically, in Vermes's generation, Renée Bloch, and, in the present age, S. Fraade. For the present argument Vermes suffices, since Bloch really did not compare *midrash* [im] in any clear sense but conducted a kind of traditions-history which she called *comparative midrash*, and since Fraade so far has done the work in two completely opposite ways.

[4] *Scripture and Tradition in Judaism* (Leiden, 1961: E. J. Brill).

[5] *op. cit.*, pp. 7-10.

Vermes validates my insistence that the word *midrash* must relate to exegesis. He now makes matters turn not on themes in general but on exegesis in particular. He further proves that when I point to the non-contextual comparisons accomplished in the name of *comparative midrash,* I do not argue with an absent enemy. There is a real position, held and worked out by actual scholars in precisely the way in which I have maintained they do the work. Vermes does hold that the same interpretation of a scriptural story may occur in diverse documents. What is important in that fact he states explicit. We therefore can investigate the time, circumstance, even determinant or precipitant of the change. Then when I point out that *comparative midrash* ignores the documentary context, treating all. statements about the same verse without regard to the preferences and distinctive traits and viewpoints of the document in which they occur, I do not set up a straw man. This view is carried on by scholars in their everyday work. And, as I have argued, it is wrong. Vermes proceeds:

> In short, RENEE BLOCH demands that midrashic literature should be studied according to the same principles of historical and literary criticism as is the Bible itself. The aim and method of such a study are expounded in an impressive fashion in her Note [cited above]....
>
> In order to classify and to date traditions, she proposed that, in addition to the employment of historical and philological criteria, etc., analysis should proceed in two stages; by means of external and internal comparison. In her view, external comparison consists in confronting Rabbinic writings recording undated traditions with non-Rabbinic Jewish texts which are at least approximately dated. These external criteria should be sought in Hellenistic Jewish works, the pseudepigrapha, Pseudo-Philo, Josephus, glosses in the Bible, the ancient Versions, the Dead Sea Scrolls, the New Testament, ancient Christian writings deriving their inspiration from Jewish sources, (e.g., Origen, Aphraates, Ephrem, etc.) and in the ancient Jewish liturgy.... Internal comparison, on the other hand, follows the development of a tradition within the boundaries of Rabbinic literature itself. The biblical text must afford the point of departure because it is the object of study, prayer, teaching, and preaching. Does R. Bloch's working hypothesis actually work? And how? Her intuition concerning the importance of the Palestinian Targum has, on the whole, been found exact in a recent study by P. Grelot. This cannot, however, be considered conclusive, and in the present book I mean to carry the test a stage further with four problems of general importance in mind:
>
> 1) the origin and development of exegetical symbolism;
>
> 2) the structure and purpose of the re-writing of the Bible;
>
> 3) the historical bond between the Bible and its interpretation;
>
> 4) the impact of theology on exegesis, and vice versa.
>
> At the same time, each chapter is intended to illustrate various methods by which problems of interpretation may be tackled.

This study is essentially devoted to Jewish exegesis, but the last two sections will also contribute, I hope, towards a sounder understanding of some fundamental questions relative to both Old and New Testaments alike.

Vermes makes explicit the grounds for joining the diverse occurrences of an exegetical program into a single composite. He makes matters explicit when he states, "The biblical text must afford the point of departure because it is the object of study, prayer, teaching, and preaching." I cannot imagine a more specific explanation of what is at issue. The studies that Vermes carries on then move in the directions dictated by his premise about the self-evident choice of the biblical text as the point of departure -- by which he means, further, the point of differentiation, comparison, and analysis -- the exegetical fulcrum. And that yields precisely that ahistorical formalism, that anti-contextual cataloguing of uninterpreted coincidences, that for me yield mere facts, but for him produce information on the topics he lists:

"2) the structure and purpose of the re-writing of the Bible; 3) the historical bond between the Bible and its interpretation; 4) the impact of theology on exegesis, and vice versa."

Once more, therefore, I point out that my characterization of *comparative midrash* as presently practiced constitutes no mere caricature but an accurate portrait of a field as it is carried on.

Let me then ask two questions. Can it be that Vermes really wishes us to ignore the documentary setting in which an exegesis occurs? Does he propose paying attention only to the exegesis and the date of the document in which it occurs, without further attention to what the compilers or authorship of the document wished to accomplish by making use of the saying or exegesis? Indeed so. Here too I have not misrepresented his position that the sole fact *about* the documentary context that matters is the date of the document. In this Vermes remains well within the program of traditions-history enunciated by Bloch. We have yet another statement in which Vermes underlines what he regards as the validity of asking Scripture itself to justify simply collecting and comparing exegeses of Scripture. Vermes further states:

Interpreters of the Hebrew Bible cannot fail to benefit from the work of their predecessors in antiquity. Not only will they discover which biblical texts were thought to demand particular interpretation: they will also notice that the midrashist's problems often coincide with their own, and may be surprised to see that 'modern' solutions to scriptural difficulties are not infrequently foreshadowed in these ancient writings. But beyond any immediate exegetical assistance, midrash is by nature apt to provide the closest historical link with Old Testament tradition itself. Scholars not misled by the analytical tendency of the literary-critical

school will fully appreciate the importance of primitive midrash to a
proper understanding of the spirit in which scripture was compiled.

The historian of the legal, social and religious ideas of post-biblical
Judaism, seeking to make decisive progress towards a reconstruction of
their complicated evolution, will in his turn find in Bible exegesis *that
precious thread of Ariadne which will lead him safely through the literary
labyrinth of Targum, Midrash, Mishnah and Talmud. He will also
discover there the unifying bond which ties biblical and post-biblical
Judaism together.*[6]

The words that I have italicized vindicate my insistence on what is at issue. But
Vermes proceeds to state his larger theological program, and it turns out to
derive from New Testament scholarship [!]:

There, too, lies the answer to a great many real problems
confronting the New Testament scholar. Since the Christian kerygma
was first formulated by Jews for Jews, using Jewish arguments and
methods of exposition, it goes without saying that a thorough
knowledge of contemporary Jewish exegesis is essential to the
understanding (and not just a better understanding) of the message of the
New Testament and, even more, of Jesus.

Comparative midrash indeed! In this statement Vermes reveals the underlying
program that he, Bloch and others attempted: a restatement of the theological
situation of the foundation of Christianity, an insistence upon the Judaism of
Christianity. That point of insistence, full of rich opportunities for
contemporary religious reconciliation, bears no scholarly motive whatsoever:
why, in descriptive terms, should anyone care? In fact *comparative midrash* in
its present formulation forms a subdiscipline of irenics, now extended even to
Judaism.

IV

What Is Wrong with
Comparative *Midrash* Today

The proponents of *comparative midrash* in its present formulation argue
quite reasonably that they too begin with a premise of shared traits. They
maintain that compare not apples and Australians but apples and apples. My
view is that they have selected the wrong traits, and that therefore they do not
describe the right things at all. They ordinarily describe and then compare [3] the
results of exegesis of a given verse in one document with [3] the results of
exegesis of that same verse in another place. By contrast I have argued that the
correct thing to describe and compare first is [2] the document that contains the

---

6 "Bible and Midrash: Early Old Testament Exegesis," in P. R. Ackroyd and C. F. Evans, eds.,
Cambridge History of the Bible (Cambridge, 1970: University Press), pp. 228-231,

results of the exegesis of diverse verses of Scripture with [2] another such document, so that comparison begins by comparing one whole document with another document, described in the way the first has been described. The present practitioners of *comparative midrash* produce information of this sort: on a given verse, X says this and Y says something else. That, sum and substance is the result of their study of *comparative midrash*. What then defines that shared foundation that makes possible comparison and contrast? As I said, it is [3] the object of *midrash*, namely as verse of Scripture.

Now to advance the argument another step. The proponents of *comparative midrash* invoke the continuity of Scripture in defense of comparing and contrasting only [3] the results of exegesis. They maintain that what one party says about a given verse of Scripture surely is comparable with what another party says about that same verse of Scripture. So they compare and contrast what two or more parties say about a given verse or story of Scripture. That seems to me entirely correct and proper, -- but only in its appropriate setting. And what is that setting at which it is quite proper to undertake comparison of [3] diverse results of exegesis and even [1] modes of exegesis? It is when we know *the setting* in which people reached one conclusion and not some other. That is to say, when we know the issues exegetes addressed and the intellectual and political and theological setting in which they did their work, then the fact that they said one thing and not something else will illuminate what they said and may further explain their rejection of what they did not say. Since, moreover, we deal not with the gist of what people said but with a given version in one set of words rather than some other, a message captured in particular language governed by conventions of form, comparison of modes of expression and conventions of language and form proceeds apace. So comparing what people said demands that we notice, also, the different ways in which they may (or may not) have said the same thing (or the opposite things). Formal traits, involving use of language and highly formalized expression, define part of the task of interpreting what is like and what is unlike.

Everything we propose to examine finds its original place in some document, rather than in some other (or in two or three documents and not in ten or twenty others). Have the framers or compilers of one document selected an item merely because that item pertains to a given verse of Scripture? Or have they chosen that item because it says what they wish to say in regard to a verse of Scripture they have identified as important? Have they framed matters in terms of their larger program of the formalization of language, syntax and rhetoric alike? Have their selection and formalization of the item particular relevance to the context in which they did their work, the purpose for which they composed their document, the larger message they planned to convey to those to whom they planned to speak? These questions demand answers, and the answers will tell us the "*what else*," that is, what is important about what people say in common or in contrast about the verse at hand. Without the answers provided by analysis of circumstance and context, plan and program, of the several documents one by one and then in comparison and contrast with one another, we know only what people said about the verse. But we do not know why they said it, what they meant by what they said, or what we learn from the fact *that* they said what they said about the verse in hand. The answers to these questions constitute that "what-else?" that transforms catalogues of pointless facts into pointed and important propositions.

The question about the precipitant of exegesis, namely, whether it is the literary and theological context, as I maintain, or principally the contents of what is said, as proponents of *comparative midrash* in its present formulation hold, brings us to the crux of the matter.

What, precisely, constitutes the faulty category-formation before us? The premise of all that I have said is that Scripture serves a diversity of purposes and therefore cannot establish a single definitive plane of meaning, the frame of reference against which all other things constitute variables. To state matters affirmatively, in my view Scripture constitutes the neutral background, not the principal and suggestive variable. The exegetes tell us what verses of Scripture matter and what we should learn from those verses. Scripture dictates nothing but endures all things. What people tell us about the meaning of Scripture (point [3] in what has gone before) represents the outcome of the work of exegetes and not the inexorable result of the character or contents of Scripture. But our entry into the interpretation of the work of exegetes begins at point [2], namely, the books that the exegetes wrote and handed on to us. Why so? Because all exegeses of verses of Scripture come to us in the form of books or equivalent, whole documents, and little if any work of exegesis of verses of Scripture reaches us in discrete form, e.g., exegesis by exegesis (though, to be sure, some compilations of exegeses exist only in fragmentary form, but that is a different thing). So to begin at the beginning, we must start with what we have in hand: the whole composite, not the individual compositions, let alone the matter of methods by which the compositions were worked out and the composites made possible. Not only so because, as I have already said, the exegesis of a verse of Scripture contained in a composite of such exegeses may or may not have been selected and shaped to suit the purposes of the compilers of the composite of exegeses, not the ideas of the authors of the composition of exegesis. In the case of the documents I have studied at length, Sifra to Leviticus, Leviticus Rabbah and Genesis Rabbah, that is an established fact. The state of the question elsewhere has not been systematically worked out, though a few have episodically commented on details.[7]

---

[7] For example, Steven D. Fraade, "Sifre Deuteronomy 26 (ad Deut. 3:23): How Conscious the Composition?" in *Hebrew Union College Annual* 54, 1983, pp. 245-302.

V

Category Formation and Comparative Midrash

Let me now frame the issue for debate as I think it should be argued and so spell out what is wrong in the category that leads us to compare what one group says about a verse of Scripture with what another group says about that same verse:

1. Does Scripture dictate the substance of exegesis?

2. Or do exegetes dictate the sense they wish to impart to (or locate in) Scripture?

If the former, then the ground for comparison finds definition in a verse of Scripture. What X said, without regard to circumstance or even documentary context, compared with what Y said, viewed also with slight attention to canonical context and concrete literary circumstance, matters. If the latter, then canon and its components take pride of place, and what diverse persons said about a given verse of Scripture defines only a coincidence, unless proved on the basis of circumstance and context to constitute more than mere coincidence.

So I think the question must confront us. The answer to the question lies spread across the surface of the reading of Scripture in the history of the scriptural religions of the West, the Judaisms and the Christianities in perpetual contention among and between themselves about which verses of Scripture matter, and what those that matter mean. That remarkably varied history tells the story of how diverse groups of believers selected diverse verses of the Hebrew Scriptures as particularly important. They then subjected those verses, and not other verses, to particular exegetical inquiry. The meanings they found in those verses answer questions they found urgent. Scripture contributed much but dictated nothing, system -- circumstance and context-- dictated everything and selected what Scripture might contribute in *midrash*. In this context, *midrash* means the whole extant repertoire of exegeses of verses of Scripture we possess in [2] various compilations of exegeses of Scripture, made up of [3] compositions of exegesis of verses of Scripture, guided by [1] diverse hermeneutical principles of interpretation of Scripture. Since in *midrash* as just now defined, system comes first, prior to exegeses of particular verses of Scripture, all the more so prior to the hermeneutics that guides the work of exegesis, the documents that contain the system form the definitive initial classification for comparative *midrash*. System must be compared to system, not detail to detail, and, therefore, to begin with, we compare [2] compilation of exegeses to the counterpart, thus document to document. That is the correct category for comparing exegeses of verses of Scripture.

Comparative midrash as now carried on ordinarily focuses on the classification defined by the verses on which people commented, ignoring the classification -- the one of circumstance and context supplied by the document and the canon -- intended to permit inquiry into why and how people chose one set of verses rather than some other. For comparison of the results of exegeses of a given verse of Scripture ignores all questions of context and circumstance -- that is, of system. But comparison of the repertoires of verses people chose and those they ignored yields the governing insight. Before we know the answers, we have to understand the questions people addressed to Scripture. Why so? Because a group chose a repertoire of verses distinctive to itself, rarely commenting on, therefore confronting, verses important to other groups. When we deal with different groups talking about different things to different groups, what difference does it make to us that, adventitiously and not systematically, out of all systemtic context, we discover that someone reached the same conclusion as did someone else, of some other group? What else do we know if we discover such a coincidence? Parallel lines never meet, and parallel statements on the same verse may in context bear quite distinct meaning.

For instance, Pharisees appear to have found especially interesting verses in Leviticus and Numbers that failed to attract much attention from the Evangelists. Evangelists found unusually weighty verses of Scripture that the Pharisees and their heirs tended to ignore. Accordingly, Scripture forms the neutral ground.[8] It is the constant -- the letter A or the continent of Australia, in our earlier analogy. Merely because both apples and Australians originate in Australia and begin with the letter A (among much else they have in common), we know nothing else than that apples and Australians originate in Australia and begin with an A. Contending groups selected verses of Scripture important to those larger programs that, to begin with, brought them to the reading and interpretation of particular verses of Scripture. True, they may have reached the

---

[8] This observation derives from my sustained inquiry into the character of compilations of scriptural exegeses produced in late antiquity by the sages who framed the canon of Judaism. My work began with *A History of the Mishnaic Law of Purities. VII. Negaim. Sifra* (Leiden, 1975: E. J. Brill). Studies of the repertoire of verses selected by Pharisees for close reading, as well as of the relationship between Scripture and the discrete rules of the Mishnah, Mishnah-tractates one by one, and the Mishnah as a whole, went forward with the further volumes of my History of the *Mishnaic Law of Purities* (Leiden, 1975-1977: E. J. Brill) I-XXII, *Holy Things* (Leiden, 1979) I-VI, *Women* (Leiden, 1979-1980) I-V, *Appointed Times* (Leiden, 1981-1983) I-V, and *Damages* (Leiden, 1983-1985) I-V. Each study of a tractate and of a complete division worked out complete, systematic, and detailed studies of the same problem. Then in *Judaism. The Evidence of the Mishnah* (Chicago, 1981: University of Chicago Press), I presented a systematic study of the question of the choice of verses for exegesis as a whole. A still more elaborate statement of the main results of detailed analysis is presented as, "From Scripture to Mishnah. A Systematic Account," in my *Method and Meaning in Ancient Judaism. Second Series* (Chicago, 1981: Scholars Press for Brown Judaic Studies), pp. 101-214. From that point I turned to the study of sages' compilations of exegeses of Scripture viewed as whole documents, and not set into relationship either with a legal conception or with a document of law. This second inquiry leads to the points of the present article. The first such study placed into canonical context the work of compiling exegeses into documents. It is *Midrash in Context. Exegesis in Formative Judaism.*. That book is volume I of *The Foundations of Judaism. Method., Teleology, Doctrine* (Philadelphia, 1983-1985: Fortress) I-III. The next project was *The Integrity of Leviticus Rabbah. The Problem of the Autonomy of a Rabbinic Document* (Chico, 1985: Scholars Press for Brown Judaic Studies). The present essay derives its main points from the third in sequence, which is my *Comparative Midrash: The Plan and Program of Genesis Rabbah and Leviticus Rabbah* (Atlanta, 1985: Scholars Press for Brown Judaic Studies). A related study is listed below, n. 11.

same conclusions about a given verse as did other groups. But so what? Do we therefore learn what that verse of Scripture must mean? No one can imagine so. We learn little about Scripture, and still less about the diverse groups whose views, on a given verse of Scripture, happened to coincide. What is neutral conveys no insight, only what is subject to contention.

That is why the choice of a given verse of Scripture for sustained inquiry comes prior to inquiry into the meaning or message discovered in that verse of Scripture. To conclude, Scripture itself forms the undifferentiated background. It is the form, not the substance, the flesh, not the spirit. The fact that a single verse of Scripture generates diverse comments by itself therefore forms a statement of a merely formal character. It is a sequence of facts that may or may not bear meaning. That statement hardly differs in logical status from the one that Australians are different from apples because all apples have stems and no Australians have stems. True enough, but so what? What *else* do we know, when we know that apples and Australians, alike in some ways, differ in the specified way? The stress in *comparative midrash* as presently done on the (mere) formality that people are talking about the same thing (the same verse of Scripture) and are saying the same thing, or different things, about that verse of Scripture, yields long catalogues of information about what different people say about the same thing. What is at stake in making these lists, what syllogism or proposition we prove by compiling information, rarely, comes to expression. More often than not, the list is the thing. There is no "what else."

My position, as is clear, is that we compare document to document, and so, for *comparative midrash* (invoking category [2]), we compare two or more compilations of exegeses. That position, moreover, points toward the proposition of this book: the correct and generative principle for category-formation derives from the canon and its components, not from the contents of documents, homogenized into some other form category entirely. Let me now spell out the foundations of the view that the work of comparison should properly begin with the complete documents and only proceed to the components of two or more documents, set side by side for contrast and analysis through comparison. Why so? Because the work of analysis rests upon establishing first the genus, and only then the species, and the comparison of one species of one genus with another species of a different genus proves parlous indeed. For when we do otherwise and deal with a species distinct from the genus which defines its traits and establishes the context of those traits, we do not really know what we have in hand. The context of a definitive trait not having been established, we cannot know the sense and meaning of a given detail, indeed, even whether the detail by itself defines and distinguishes the species of which it is a part. It is the genus which permits us to describe and analyze the species of that genus. When, therefore, we propose to undertake a work of comparison and contrast, we must begin at the level of the genus, and not at any lesser layer. What that means is simple. The work of description, prior to analysis and so comparison and contrast, begins with the whole, and only then works its way down to the parts. The work of analysis, resting on such a labor of description, proceeds once more, as I have proposed, from the whole, the genus, to the parts, the species. Why do I maintain that the document defines the genus -- the document, and not the verse of Scripture on which people comment? The reason is both negative, namely, the miscellaneous character of the diverse exegetical traditions of Judaism and Christianity, as noted just now, but also positive. The traits of the documents themselves decide the issue. They exhibit integrity, so that their contents in detail testify to the plan and program of the compositors of the compilations of exegeses of Scripture. Let me turn to the specific document that in an exemplary way validates this judgment.

In my study of Leviticus Rabbah[9] I proposed to demonstrate in the case of that compilation of exegeses of Scripture that a rabbinic document constitutes a text, not merely a scrapbook or a random compilation of episodic materials. A text is a document with a purpose, one that exhibits the traits of the integrity of the parts to the whole and the fundamental autonomy of the whole from other texts. I showed that the document at hand therefore falls into the classification of a cogent composition, put together with purpose and intended as a whole and in the aggregate to bear a meaning and state a message. I therefore disproved the claim, for the case before us, that a rabbinic document serves merely as an anthology or miscellany or is to be compared only to a scrapbook, made up of this and that. In that exemplary instance I pointed to the improbability that a document has been brought together merely to join discrete and ready-made bits and pieces of episodic discourse. A document in the canon of Judaism thus does not merely define a context for the aggregation of such already completed and mutually distinct materials. Rather, I proved, that document constitutes a text. So at issue in my study of Leviticus Rabbah is what makes a text a text, that is, the textuality of a document. At stake is how we may know when a document constitutes a text and when it is merely an anthology or a scrapbook.

The importance of that issue for the correct method of comparison is clear. If we can show that a document is a miscellany, then traits of the document have no bearing on the contents of the document -- things that just happen to be preserved there, rather than somewhere else. If, by contrast, the text possesses its own, integrity, then everything in the text must first of all be interpreted in the context of the text, then in the context of the canon of which the text forms a constituent. Hence my stress on the comparison of whole documents, prior to the comparison of the results of exegesis contained within those documents, rests upon the result of the study of Leviticus Rabbah. Two principal issues frame the case. The first is what makes a text a text. The textuality of a text concerns whether a given piece of writing hangs together and is to be read on its own. The second is what makes a group of texts into a canon, a cogent

---

[9] Cited above, n. 8.

statement all together. At issue is the relationship of two or more texts of a single, interrelated literature to the world-view and way of life of a religious tradition viewed whole. So the documents define the categories, hence the grounds for comparison and contrast.

VI

Challenges to the Canonical Theory of Category Formation in Comparative Midrash

Now it may be claimed by proponents of the comparison of *midrash* meaning of the results of exegesis and not the documents that compile exegeses that the character of the documents supports their view, not mine. How so? They point to the fact that stories and exegeses move from document to document. The travels of a given saying or story or exegesis of Scripture from one document to another validate comparing what travels quite apart from what stays home. And that is precisely what comparing exegeses of the same verse of Scripture occurring in different settings does. The *comparative-midrashists* therefore maintain that traveling materials enjoy their own integrity, apart from the texts that quite adventitiously give them a temporary home. The problem of therefore is whether or not a rabbinic document stands by itself or right at the outset forms a scarcely differentiated segment of a larger and uniform canon, one made up of materials that travel everywhere and take up residence indifferent to the traits of their temporary abode. If documents do not stand on their own, then they also cannot constitute the correct categories for the description, analysis, and interpretation of the data they contain. There must then be some other category-formation to tell us how to approach the data. So the issue presents a critical turning in the argument.

The reason one might suppose that, in the case of the formative age of Judaism, a document does not exhibit integrity and is not autonomous is simple. The several writings of the rabbinic canon of late antiquity, formed from the Mishnah, ca. A.D. 200, through the Talmud of Babylonia, ca. A.D. 600, with numerous items in between, do share materials -- sayings, tales, protracted discussions. Some of these shared materials derive from explicitly-cited documents. For instance, passages of Scripture or of the Mishnah or of the Tosefta, cited verbatim, will find their way into the two Talmuds. But sayings, stories, and sizable compositions not identified with a given, earlier text and exhibiting that text's distinctive traits will float from one document to the next.

That fact has so impressed students of the rabbinic canon as to produce a firm consensus of fifteen hundred years' standing. It is that one cannot legitimately study one document in isolation from others, describing its rhetorical, logical, literary, and conceptual traits and system all by themselves. To the contrary, all documents contribute to a common literature, or, more accurately, religion -- Judaism. In the investigation of matters of rhetoric, logic literature, and conception, whether of law or of theology, all writings join equally to given testimony to the whole. For the study of the formative history of Judaism, the issue transcends what appears to be the simple, merely literary question at hand: when is a text a text? In the larger context of that question we return to the issue of the peripatetic sayings, stories, and exegeses.

When I frame matters in terms of the problem of the rabbinic document, I ask what defines a document as such, the text-ness, the textuality, of a text. How do we know that a given book in the canon of Judaism is something other than a scrapbook? The choices are clear. One theory is that a document serves solely as a convenient repository of prior sayings and stories, available materials that will have served equally well (or poorly) wherever they took up their final location. In accord with that theory it is quite proper in ignorance of all questions of circumstance and documentary or canonical context to compare the exegesis of a verse of Scripture in one document with the exegesis of that verse of Scripture found in some other document. The other theory is that a composition exhibits a viewpoint, a purpose of authorship distinctive to its framers or collectors and arrangers. Such a characteristic literary purpose -- by this other theory -- is so powerfully particular to one authorship that nearly everything at hand can be shown to have been (re)shaped for the ultimate purpose of the authorship at hand, that is, collectors and arrangers who demand the title of authors. In accord with this other theory context and circumstance form the prior condition of inquiry, the result, in exegetical terms, the contingent one. To resort again to a less than felicitous neologism, I thus ask what signifies or defines the "document-ness" of a document and what makes a book a book. I therefore wonder whether there are specific texts in the canonical context of Judaism or whether all texts are merely contextual. In framing the question as I have, I of course lay forth the mode of answering it. . We have to confront a single rabbinic composition, and ask about its definitive traits and viewpoint.

But we have also to confront the issue of the traveling sayings, the sources upon which the redactors of a given document have drawn. By "sources" I mean simply passages in a given book that occur, also, in some other rabbinic book. Such sources -- by definition prior to the books in which they appear -- fall into the classification of materials general to two or more compositions and by definition not distinctive and particular to any one of them. The word "source" therefore serves as an analogy to convey the notion that two or more sets of authors have made use of a single, available item. About whether or not the shared item is prior to them both or borrowed by one from the other at this stage we cannot speculate. As I said, these shared items, transcending two or more documents and even two or more complete systems or groups, if paramount and preponderant, would surely justify the claim that we may compare [3] exegeses of verses of Scripture without attention to [2] context. Why? Because there is no context defined by the limits of a given document and its characteristic plan and program. All the documents do is collect and arrange available materials.

The document does not define the context of its contents. If that can be shown, then *comparative midrash* may quite properly ignore the contextual dimension imparted to sayings, including exegeses of Scripture, by their occurrence in one document rather than some other.

Let me now summarize this phase of the argument. We ask about the textuality of a document -- is it a composition or a scrap book? -- so as to determine the appropriate foundations for comparison, the correct classifications for comparative study. We seek to determine the correct context of comparison, hence the appropriate classification.

My claim is simple: once we know what is unique to a document, we can investigate the traits that characterize all the document's unique and so definitive materials. We ask about whether the materials unique to a document also cohere, or whether they prove merely miscellaneous. If they do cohere, we may conclude that the framers of the document have followed a single plan and a program. That would in my view justify the claim that the framers carried out a labor not only of conglomeration, arrangement and selection, but also of genuine authorship or composition in the narrow and strict sense of the word. If so, the document emerges from authors, not merely arrangers and compositors. For the same purpose, therefore, we also take up and analyze the items shared between that document and some other or among several documents. We ask about the traits of those items, one by one and all in the aggregate. In these stages we may solve for the case at hand the problem of the rabbinic document: do we deal with a scrapbook or a cogent composition? A text or merely a literary expression, random and essentially promiscuous, of a larger theological context? That is the choice at hand.

Since we have reached a matter of fact, let me state the facts as they are. To begin with, I describe the relationships among the principal components of the literature with which we deal. The several documents that make up the canon of Judaism in late antiquity relate to one another in three important ways. First, all of them refer to the same basic writing, the Hebrew Scriptures. Many of them draw upon the Mishnah and quote it. So the components of the canon join at their foundations. Second, as the documents reached closure in sequence, the later authorship can be shown to have drawn upon earlier, completed documents. So the writings of the rabbis of the talmudic corpus accumulate and build from layer to layer. Third, as I have already hinted, among two or more documents some completed units of discourse, and many brief, discrete sayings, circulated, for instance, sentences or episodic homilies or fixed apothegms of various kinds. So in some (indeterminate) measure the several documents draw not only upon one another, as we can show, but also upon a common corpus of materials that might serve diverse editorial and redactional purposes.

The extent of this common corpus can never be fully known. We know only what we have, not what we do not have. So we cannot say what has been omitted, or whether sayings that occur in only one document derive from materials available to the editors or compilers of some or all other documents. That is something we never can know. We can describe only what is in our hands and interpret only the data before us. Of indeterminates and endless speculative possibilities we need take no account. In taking up documents one by one, do we not obscure their larger context and their points in common?

In fact, shared materials proved for Leviticus Rabbah not many and not definitive. They form an infinitesimal proportion of Genesis Rabbah, under 3-5% of the volume of the parashiyyot for which I conducted probes.[10]. Materials that occur in both Leviticus Rabbah and some other document prove formally miscellany and share no single viewpoint or program; they are random and brief. What is unique to Leviticus Rabbah and exhibits that document's characteristic formal traits also predominates and bears the message of the whole. So much for the issue of the peripatetic exegesis. To date I have taken up the issue of homogeneity of "sources,"in a limited and mainly formal setting, for the matter of how sayings and stories travel episodically from one document to the next.[11] The real issue is not the traveling, but the unique, materials: the documents, and not what is shared among them. The variable -- what moves -- is subject to analysis only against the constant: the document itself.

VII

Canon and Comparison

Let me now spell out why I think the correct category is defined by the document of a given canon, which is to be described, analyzed, and interpreted, so that, in addition, we may properly and therefore in context understand the exegeses of Scripture contained in that document. The activity of scriptural exegesis constituted a cultural commonplace, a prevailing convention of thought, and therefore by itself cannot yield points of differentiation. Bases for analysis, comparison, and contrast derive from points of differentiation, not sameness. Comparing what unrelated groups said about the same matter tells us only facts, not their meaning. But the purpose of comparison is interpretation. We might as well attempt to differentiate within diverse ages and formulations of Israelite culture on the basis of so commonplace an activity as writing books or eating bread. True enough, diverse groups wrote diverse books, and, we might imagine, also baked their bread in diverse ways, e.g., with or without yeast, with wheat, or barley, or rye. But so what? Only if we can show that people did

---

[10] There were two kinds of exceptions. First, entire *parashiyyot* occur in both Leviticus Rabbah and, verbatim, in Pesiqta der. Kahana. Second, Genesis Rabbah and Leviticus Rabbah share sizable compositions. The former sort always conform to the formal program of Leviticus Rabbah. They in no way stand separate from the larger definitive and distinctive traits of the document. The latter sort fit quite comfortably, both formally and programmatically, into both Genesis Rabbah and Leviticus Rabbah, because those two documents themselves constitute species of a single genus, as I shall point out below.

[11] *The Peripatetic Saying. The Problem of the Thrice-Told Tale in Talmudic Literature* (Chico, 1985).

these things as a mode of expressing ideas particular to themselves, their condition and context, can we answer the question, so what? That is why comparing merely what people said about the same thing, whether the weather or the meaning of Genesis 49:10, without regard to the circumstance in which they said it, meaning, in our case, to begin with the particular book and canon in which what they said is now preserved, produces knowledge of a merely formal character. Let me now spell this out, since we cannot understand how *comparative midrash* has been carried on to this time without a clear picture of its false premise as to category-formation and classification.

Midrash, meaning exegesis of Scripture, by itself presents nothing new in Israelite culture. Explaining the verses of holy books, even before the formation of the Holy Book, went on routinely. Why what diverse groups said about the same verse would form a consequential area of comparative study therefore demands explanation, for the answer is not self-evident.

We need not hunt at length for evidence of the work of collecting exercises in exegesis -- of rewriting an old text in light of new considerations or values. Such a vast enterprise is handsomely exemplified by the book of Chronicles which, instead of merely commenting on verses, actually rewrites the stories of Samuel and Kings. Anyone who without attention to the larger documentary context -- the respective programs of the compilations as a whole -- compares what the compilers of Samuel and Kings say about a given incident with what the compilers of Chronicles say about the same incident then misses the point of the difference between the reading of the one and that of the other. For, as everyone now knows, the difference derives from the documentary context -- there alone. So without asking first of all about the plan and program of the documents, the formal comparison of contents produces facts, but no insight into their meaning. That, in my view, is the present situation of comparative midrash.

When people wished to deliver a powerful argument for a basic proposition, they did so by collecting and arranging exegeses of Scripture -- and, it goes without saying, also by *producing* appropriate exegeses of Scripture for these compilations. That is to say, compilers also participated in the framing or rewriting of what they compiled, so that all we have is what they chose to give us in the language and form they selected. That is why I maintain study of *comparative midrash* must begin with the outermost point of contact, namely, the character of the compilation of exegeses. Comparing one compilation with another then defines the first stage of the comparison of exegeses: compilations, contents, principles of hermeneutics alike. To gain perspective on this proposition, we now turn to two fairly systematic efforts at compiling exegeses of Scripture specifically in order to make some polemical point. These show how compilers and exegetes made their collections of exegeses in order to demonstrate propositions critical to their theological program. We detect here little that was wholly random in either proposition or proportion, selection and arrangement of exegeses or propositions on the meaning of specific verses of Scripture. All aspects -- mode of exegesis, result of exegesis, purpose of compilation alike -- address the point of the document as a whole, carrying out the established purpose. They demonstrate the unity of form and meaning, of purpose and proposition. The selection of exegeses, the creation of exegeses, the arrangement and compilation of exegeses, the use of a particular formal technique, and the larger polemic or theological proposition that motivated the compilers and exegetes alike -- all of these together join in producing the document as we know it. Therefore we compare document to document, not uninterpreted detail ripped from one document to an equivalent detail seized from some other. We ask two questions.

We turn first to two passages of exegesis, one of Hosea, the other of Nahum, found in the Essene Library of Qumran. As presented by Geza Vermes,[12] the exegeses do form something we might call a collection, or at least a chapter, that is, a systematic treatment of a number of verses in sequence. Vermes's presentation is a follows:

Commentary on Hosea

In this interpretation, the unfaithful wife is the Jewish people, and her lovers are the Gentiles who have led the nation astray.

"[She knew not that] it was I who gave her [the new wine and oil], who lavished [upon her silver] and gold which they [used for Baal]" (2:8).

Interpreted, this means that [they ate and] were filled, but they forgot God who.... They cast His commandments behind them which He had sent [by the hand of] His servants the Prophets, and they listened to those who led them astray. They revered them, and in their blindness they feared them as though they were gods.

"Therefore I will take back my corn in its time and my wine [in its season]. I will take away my wool and my flax lest they cover [her nakedness]. I will uncover her shame before the eyes of [her] lovers [and] no man shall deliver her from out of my hand" (2:9-10).

Interpreted, this means that He smote them with hunger and nakedness that they might be shamed and disgraced in the sight of the nations on which they relied. They will not deliver them from their miseries.

"I will put an end to her rejoicing, [her feasts], her [new] moons, her Sabbaths, and all her festivals" (2:11).

Interpreted, this means that [they have rejected the ruling of the law, and have] followed the festivals of the nations. But [their rejoicing shall come to an end and] shall be changed into mourning.

---

[12] *The Dead Sea Scrolls in English* (Harmondsworth, 1975), 230-33.

I will ravage [her vines and her fig trees], of which she said, 'They are my wage [which my lovers have given me]'. I will make of them a thicket and the [wild beasts] shall eat them...." (2:12).

On the Commentary on Nahum, Vermes comments: "For a correct understanding of the interpretation of Nahum 2:12, the reader should bear in mind the biblical order that only the corpses of executed criminals should be hanged (Deut. 21:21). Hanging men alive, i.e., crucifixion, was a sacrilegious novelty. Some translators consider the mutilated final sentence unfinished, and render it: 'For a man hanged alive on a tree shall be called...' The version given here seems more reasonable. The passage is as follows:

"[Where is the lions' den and the cave of the young lions?]" (2:11).

[Interpreted, this concerns]...a dwelling-place for the ungodly of the nations.

"Whither the lion goes, there is the lion's cub, [with none to disturb it]" (2:11b).

[Interpreted, this concerns Deme]trius king of Greece who sought, on the counsel of those who seek smooth things, to enter Jerusalem. [But God did not permit the city to be delivered] into the hands of the kings of Greece, from the time of Antiochus until the coming of the rulers of the Kittim. But then she shall be trampled under their feet....

"The lion tears enough for its cubs and it chokes prey for its lionesses" (2:12a).

[Interpreted, this] concerns the furious young lion who strikes by means of his great men, and by means of the men of his council.

"[And chokes prey for its lionesses; and it fills] its caves [with prey] and its dens with victims" (2:12a-b).

Interpreted, this concerns the furious young lion [who executes revenge] on those who seek smooth things and hangs men alive, [a thing never done] formerly in Israel. Because of a man hanged alive on [the] tree, He proclaims, "Behold I am against [you, says the Lord of Hosts]."

"[I will burn up your multitude in smoke], and the sword shall devour your young lions. I will [cut off] your prey [from the earth]" (2:13):

[Interpreted]..."your multitude" is the bands of his army...and his "young lions" are...his "prey" is the wealth which [the priests] of Jerusalem have [amassed], which...Israel shall be delivered....

"[And the voice of your messengers shall no more be heard]" (2:13b).

[Interpreted]...his "messengers" are his envoys whose voice shall no more he heard among the nations.

Treating the materials presented by Vermes as a document, we simply cannot categorize these several "units of discourse" within the framework of taxonomy suitable for, e.g., Genesis Rabbah and Leviticus Rabbah. For we do not have (1) a word-for-word or point-by-point reading, in light of other verses of Scripture, of the verses that are cited, let alone (2) an expansion on the topics of the verses. The forms serving the two Rabbah-compilations obviously do not apply. What we have is an entirely different sort of exegesis, given in an entirely different form, namely, a reading of the verses of Scripture in light of an available scheme of concrete events. The exegete wishes to place into relationship to Scripture things that have happened in his own day. His form serves that goal.

If the generative principle of exegesis seems alien, the criterion of composition as a whole is entirely familiar. The compiler wished to present amplifications of the meaning of a verse of Scripture, not word-for-word or phrase-for-phrase interpretations. He also has not constructed a wide-ranging discussion of the theme of the verse such as we noted in the more philosophical taxon (III), let alone a mere anthology (A). Let me with appropriate emphasis state the main point.

The framer of the passage selected a mode of constructing his unit of discourse wholly congruent with the purpose for which, to begin with, he undertook the exegesis of the passage.

He wished to read the verses of Scripture in light of events. So he organized his unit of discourse around the sequence of verses of Scripture under analysis. Had he wanted, he might have provided a sequential narrative of what happened, then inserting the verse he found pertinent, thus: "X happened, and that is the meaning of (biblical verse) Y." (Such a mode of organizing exegeses served the school of Matthew, but not the framer of the text at hand. I do not know why). In any event the construction at hand is rather simple. The far more complex modes of constructing units of discourse in Genesis Rabbah and Leviticus Rabbah served a different purpose. They are made up, moreover, of different approaches to the exegesis of Scripture. So we see that the purpose of exegesis makes a deep impact upon not only the substance of the exegesis, but also, and especially, upon the formal and redactional characteristics of the document, the mode of organizing the consequent collection of exegeses.

Obviously, there were diverse ways both of undertaking scriptural exegesis and of organizing the collections of such exegeses. In the setting of examples of these other ways in which earlier Jews had responded to verses of Scripture and then collected and organized their responses, we see that there was more than a single compelling way in which to do the work. It represented a distinctive choice among possibilities others in Israelite culture had explored It may now be fairly argued that the rather episodic sets of exegeses presented to us by the Essene library of Qumran cannot be called documents and compared to the sustained and purposeful labor of both exegesis and composition revealed in the earliest rabbinic collections. Accordingly, in conclusion let us turn, for a second exercise of comparison, to an exegetical passage exhibiting clear-cut and fixed forms of rhetoric, both of the exegetical passage itself, and of the composition of several exegetical passages into a large-scale discourse -- hence, units of discourse to be compared with units of discourse of Genesis Rabbah. We find in the literary composition of the school of Matthew a powerful effort to provide an interpretation of verses of Scripture in line with a distinct program of interpretation. Furthermore, the selection and arrangement of these scriptural exegeses turn out to be governed by the large-scale purpose of the framers of the document as a whole.

To illustrate these two facts, I present four parallel passages, in which we find a narrative, culminating in the citation of a verse of Scripture, hence a convention of formal presentation of ideas, style and composition alike. In each case, the purpose of the narrative is not only fulfilled in itself, but also in a subscription linking the narrative to the cited verse and stating explicitly that the antecedent narrative serves to fulfill the prediction contained in the cited verse, hence a convention of theological substance. We deal with Matthew 1:18-23, 2:1-6, 2:16-18, and 3:1-3.

Mt. 1:18-23

Now the birth of Jesus Christ took place in this way. When his mother Mary had been betrothed to Joseph, before they came together she was found to be with child of the Holy Spirit; and her husband Joseph, being a just man and unwilling to put her to shame, resolved to divorce her quietly. But as he considered this, behold, an angel of the Lord appeared to him in a dream, saying, "Joseph, son of David, do not fear to take Mary your wife, for that which is conceived in her is of the Holy Spirit; she will bear a son, and you shall call his name Jesus, for he will save his people from their sins." All this took place to fulfill what the Lord had spoken by the prophet: "Behold, a virgin shall conceive and bear a son, and his name shall be called Emmanuel" (which means, God with us).

Mt. 2:1-6

Now when Jesus was born in Bethlehem of Judea in the days of Herod the king, behold, wise men from the East came to Jerusalem, saying, "Where is he who has been born king of the Jews? For we have seen his star in the East, and have come to worship him." When Herod the king heard this, he was troubled, and all Jerusalem with him; and assembling all the chief priests and scribes of the people, he inquired of them where the Christ was to be born. They told him, "In Bethlehem of Judea; for so it is written by the prophet: "And you, O Bethlehem, in the land of Judah, are by no means least among the rulers of Judah; for from you shall come a ruler who will govern my people Israel.'"

Mt. 2:16-18

    Then Herod, when he saw that he had been tricked by the wise men, was in a furious rage, and he sent and killed all the male children in Bethlehem and in all that region who were two years old or under, according to the time which he had ascertained from the wise men. Then was fulfilled what was spoken by the prophet Jeremiah: "A voice was heard in Ramah, wailing and loud lamentation, Rachel weeping for her children; she refused to be consoled, because they were no more."

Mt. 3:1-3

    In those days came John the Baptist, preaching in the wilderness of Judea, "Repent, for the kingdom of heaven is at hand." For this is he who was spoken of by the prophet Isaiah when he said, "The voice of one crying in the wilderness: Prepare the way of the Lord, make his paths straight."

    The four passages show us a stunningly original mode of linking exegeses. The organizing principle derives from the sequence of events of a particular biography, rather than the sequence of verses in a given book of Scripture or of sentences of the Mishnah. The biography of the person under discussion serves as the architectonic of the composition of exegeses into a single statement of meaning. This mode of linking exegeses -- that is, composing them into a large-scale collection, such as we have at hand in the earliest rabbinic compilations -- shows us another way than the way taken at Qumran, on the one side, and among the late fourth and fifth centuries' compilers of rabbinic collections of exegeses, on the other.

    The passages of Matthew, therefore, indicate a clear-cut, distinctive choice on how to compose a "unit of discourse" and to join several congruent units of discourse into a sustained statement, a document. The choice is dictated by the character and purpose of the composition at hand. Since the life of a particular person -- as distinct from events of a particular character -- forms the focus of discourse, telling a story connected with that life and following this with a citation of the biblical verse illustrated in the foregoing story constitutes the generative and organizing principle of the several units of discourse, all of them within a single taxon. The taxon is not only one-dimensional. It also is rather simple in both its literary traits and its organizing principle. We discern extremely tight narration of a tale, followed by a citation of a verse of Scripture, interpreted only through the device of the explicit joining language: This (1) is what that (2) means. What we see so clearly in the work of the school of Matthew is a simple fact. The work of making up exegeses of Scripture, selecting the appropriate ones and saying important things about them, and the labor of collecting and compiling these exegeses of Scripture into a larger composite together express a single principle, make a single statement, carry out the purposes of a single polemic. Let me once more give proper emphasis to this simple result:

Three things go together: (1) the principles of exegesis, (2) the purposes of exegesis, and (3) the program of collecting and arranging exegeses into compilations.

That is the fact of Matthew. It is true of Sifra.[13] I have tried to demonstrate that it is the fact of Genesis Rabbah and Leviticus Rabbah as well. In time to come, detailed analysis of the various compilations of biblical exegeses produced at diverse places and times within Judaism, from the fifth century to the eighteenth, will tell us whether or not it is so later on as well.

So we see a simple fact. First, what people wished to say about the meaning of a verse of Scripture and, second, why they then proposed to collect what they had said into cogent compositions -- these two considerations cohere. When we can say in connection with other compilations of scriptural exegeses what we think generated comments on biblical verses, and how composing these particular comments on these selected verses into compilations or compositions made sense to composers, we shall be well on the way to describing, analyzing, and interpreting the context -- the life-situation -- of those documents, hence also to the comparison of document to document, one whole compilation of exegeses of Scripture with another whole compilation, that is, *comparative midrash* the way comparison should begin, that is to say, by comparing with one another the appropriate categories of things.[14] What follows for our inquiry hardly requires restatement: if the document is the thing, then the canon is the source. The principle of category-formation begins with the Torah.

---

[13] Cf. *Purities. VI. Negaim. Sifra,* cited above.

[14] I repeat: begin, but not conclude. The other dimensions of exegesis, compilation, and hermeneutics also demand comparative and analytical study.

Chapter Three

Interpretation:
The Category "Messianism"

I

The Messianic Idea in Judaism?

The generative category, *Judaism*, directs us to appropriate, and inappropriate, evidence for the description of Judaism. It tells us at what points to differentiate -- thus creating new categories -- and at what points to treat data as a unity and to underline their harmony and homogeneity. So, read as a group, all of the writings of Jews in late antiquity testify to Judaism. If, then, we take a given subtopic or category to these same sources, the writings we deem canonical will tell us what that same Judaism says about the topic at hand. Thus if we take all the available writings all together and all at once, we may describe the idea of Judaism about a given topic. Read not all together all at once, but one by one, however, the synagogue writings and rabbinic canon yield no such thing as, e.g., *the* messianic idea.[1] As we shall see, they yield diverse bits and pieces of information -- ways in which to this group or that author the Messiah-theme proves serviceable. So if we did not know in advance that there was a single encompassing category, "Judaism," to which all sources without differentiation testify, we also could never have formed the category, Messianism, within that Judaism. On the other hand, as is clear from the works cited above, if we do posit a single, generative and encompassing category, *Judaism*, we also may turn to all sources equally and ask them to tell us the doctrine on the Messiah presented by Judaism. So when we ask about the Messiah-idea, we come to another occasion for the testing of the received modes of category-formation and their consequent categories.

How shall we test the category, "Judaism," by analyzing its sub-category, "the Messianic Idea in Judaism"? One way of testing the viability of a category

---

[1] Bibliography:

Joseph Klausner, *The Messianic Idea in Israel: From its Beginning to the Completion of the Mishnah* (New York, 1955: Macmillan). Translated from the third Hebrew Edition by W.F. Stinespring.

Gershom Scholem, *The Messianic Idea in Judaism and Other Essays on Jewish Spirituality* (N.Y., 1971: Schocken Books). In particular, "Toward an Understanding of the Messianic Idea in Judaism," pp. 1-36.

is to ask whether it facilitates or impedes the accurate description of data. Let me spell out this (somewhat self-serving) criterion. Essentially, my test consists in asking that we try one approach and then its opposite and see the result. Our criterion for evaluating results is simple: if we do things in two different ways, do we see the evidence with greater or with less perspicacity? That somewhat subjective criterion will rapidly prove its value. So let us conduct an experiment in our imagination.

If a category does not differentiate, then we ask what happens if we do differentiate. If it does differentiate, we ask what happens if we do not. These are simple research experiments, which anyone can replicate. To spell them out also poses no great difficulty. If differentiating yields results we should have missed had we not read the documents one by one, then our category has obscured important points of difference. If *not* differentiating yields a unity that differentiating has obscured, so that the parts appear, seen all together, to cohere, then the category that has required differentiation has obscured important points in common. How shall we know one way or the other? Do we not invoke a subjective opinion when we conclude that there is, or is not, a unity that differentiation has obscured? I think not. In fact the operative criterion is superficial and self-evident, a matter of fact and not subjective judgment.

If we find that each one of the documents says on its own essentially what all of the documents say together, so that the parts do turn out to be interchangeable, then our category that imposes distinctions suggests differences where there is none. The parts not only add up to the sum of the whole, as in the case of a homogenizing category. Each of the parts replicates the fundamental structure of the whole. In that case, differentiation proves misleading.

If, by contrast, when viewed one by one, our documents in fact do not say the same thing by themselves that all of them say when read together, our category, failing to recognize differences, suggests a unity and a cogency where there is none. The parts may well add up to the sum of the whole, but each of the parts appears to stand by itself and does not replicate the statement to which, as part of a larger whole, it contributes. In that case, not effecting a considerable labor of description of the documents one by one will obscure the very center and heart of matters: that the documents, components of the whole, are themselves autonomous, though connected (if that can be shown) and also continuous (if that can be shown).

Accordingly, the results of an experiment of differentiation where, up to now, everything has been read as a single harmonious statement, a doctrine, "The Messiah-Idea in Judaism," will prove suggestive -- an interesting indicator of the effect and usefulness of the category at hand. Since, in the case of "the Messianic idea in Judaism," we treat all writings produced by all Jews as essentially homologous testimonies to a single encompassing Judaism, we shall now engage in a hitherto-neglected exercise of differentiation. We ask what each source produced by Jews in late antiquity, read by itself, has to say about the subject at hand. And when we listen to each source by itself, we have further to ask how what the document says about the Messiah relates to what it says about a variety of other subjects -- its message or polemic or viewpoint as a whole, if we can demonstrate that there was an encompassing polemic in the document and that it is not merely a scrapbook (a point we shall pursue in Chapter Four). That, after all, is the argument in connection with the analytical processes of comparison and contrast. Our category must emerge from the data, and the first category -- generated inductively out of the data -- is the data's own category, which is, the document. So that is where we start here too.

How shall we differentiate among the available writings? I take as a simple point the life-situation addressed by the various documents, and that at the most superficial level: synagogue as against school. Synagogue writings are those that, it is unanimously held, served the purposes of public worship, and these are two: the liturgical writings assigned to late antiquity and the Targumim, translations of Scripture into Aramaic, which, it is generally held, were read aloud in the synagogue for popular edification. School-writings are those that -- again, by general agreement -- derived from and proved serviceable among masters and disciples.

Once we differentiate among types of a given canon of sources, we do discover distinctions among assertions about the Messiah. More important, we discern quite diverse ways in which the Messiah myth serves these several compositions. It follows that the conception of a single prevailing construct, to which all assertions about the Messiah by definition testify, does not exist. When we look at the origins of statements about the Messiah (as about any other topic), we turn out to "deconstruct" what has been invented whole and complete in our time. Books on the Messianic Idea in Judaism by Klausner and Scholem provide portraits of a composite that, in fact, never existed in any one book, time, or place, or even in the imagination of any one social group, except an imagined "Israel" or a made-up "Judaism."[2] So once we distinguish one type or system of Judaism or one group of Israelites from another, recognizing commonalities and underscoring points of difference, we no longer find it possible to describe and analyze the messianic idea at all. Indeed, in the present context, we can no longer even comprehend the parallel categories, *the idea of* --- and --- *in Judaism*. The upshot is that a new classification is required and new categories must be defined. These appear, I shall suggest in Chapter Four, in two ways. First, they emerge from the differences between one book and another, related book in the same canon. Second, they arise from the recognition

---

[2]The category Israel serves, so it seems, just as does Judaism, as a mode of homogenization and harmonization. But study of the uses of that category, a problem in contemporary theology, as well as of the sources that are identified as appropriate, and inapppropriate, for the study of that category, remains at the most primitive stage. I cannot point to a single work of solid judgment and sophistication on the subject. For what there is, see the dreadful Lawrence H. Schiffman, *Who Was a Jew?* (Hoboken, 1985: Ktav).

that categories of books reflect different life situations. Both of these types of categories form commonplaces in contemporary learning.

How diverse groups make use of a single idea indicates ways in which each group takes shape and differs from others. What is shared in common places into perspective what differentiates one from the next. Points of insistence important in one setting but not in some other adumbrate differentiating and definitive traits of the setting in which they matter. These self-evident principles of defining a species by distinguishing it from other species of the same genus work under one condition. We have to begin with to recognize that the genus at hand is differentiated among a number of species. Then we may go in search of points of comparison and contrast. In that quest we may see more clearly why a given species exhibits the definitive characteristics that it does and how these same characteristics among themselves fit together into a cogent whole. When (to revert to the argument of Chapter One) we take up the study of Judaism in the first seven centuries of the Common Era, the labor of differentiating "Judaisms among Judaism," that is, species within the genus, begins in our own time. Heretofore people have taken all documents generally held to be Judaic and all archaeological evidence produced by Jews and indiscriminately joined all the bits and pieces, without regard to origin, into a single composite "Judaism." But that is to accomplish at the outset what should be done -- if done at all -- only at the very end. And I maintain that those who seek not to describe Judaisms but to define Judaism do so only for theological, not academic, purposes.

So, to conclude the argument: What happens if we ask about how a given document hangs together on its own? What do we discover when we read a single composition as if it was for a clear-cut purpose that someone made it as we have it. We see the components one by one and describe the traits of each. Then we have the possibility of showing how the diverse elements that ultimately cohered as Judaism in fact took shape. We may gain a picture not only of the whole, but also of the historical and philosophical processes as these were under way, each on its own, prior to aggregation into a whole. Then, but only then, we may hope for a perception not only of an idea as it finally emerged whole, but of the history of an idea at various times and in diverse places or circles in which a given composition was written down. And, I underline, we may further raise too-long-postponed questions about the relationship between the formation of ideas and the history and the society in which that process of formation took place. When we know how content related to context, how the substance of rabbinic thought responded to the situation in which rabbis and other Jews found themselves, we may explain how Judaism as we know it took shape. That is to say, we may begin to form a hypothesis about the history of Judaism in its formative stages.

Theorizing on such large questions lies in the long future. Up to now the work of parsing ideas along the lines of the documents in which they make their appearance has reached only its earliest stages. Not only so, but distinguishing ideas as they come to expression in one type of literature, or in one social context, from those same ideas as they reach articulation in some other type of writing or of social context, -- that work of differentiation, so far as I know, begins here. What I propose, specifically, is to work with universally accepted facts in order to ask how a given idea makes its appearance in two distinct, though interrelated, social settings, as these settings are represented for us in literature deemed characteristic of each of the two settings, respectively.

I propose, concretely, to examine what people say about the topic of the Messiah in two distinct types of ancient Jewish religious writings. The first is those associated with the synagogue, the second, those associated with the circle of masters and disciples we call disciples of sages, or, using the honorific anachronistically assigned as distinctive to them, rabbis.

In the category of synagogue-writings, everyone agrees, are three: *Targumim, Siddur,* and *piyyutim* (explained presently).

In the classification of rabbinical writings, it is universally acknowledged, are the Mishnah, Tosefta, two Talmuds, and exegetical works of Scripture ("*midrashim*") associated with them. There is considerable disagreement on the status of the *midrash*-compositions. The scholarly consensus of the past century that these served to write down synagogue-sermons now comes into serious question. We therefore shall not pay detailed attention to those documents at all.

What I propose is to ask what people have to say about the Messiah in documents that, all concur, derive from the synagogue, and whether what they have to say is pretty much the same thing as, or surely quite another thing than, what people have to say about the Messiah in documents that emerge from the life-situation of the master-disciple-circle. In this brief review of the literature, parsed in the way I have outlined, we gain the possibility of seeing whether, in fact, making the distinction at hand produces a substantial difference, and, if so, what that difference might be.

Two social-institutional settings produced the extant writings of ancient Judaism under discussion here: the school and the synagogue. (There are numerous other types of writings produced by Jews in late antiquity, whose life-situation remains to be analyzed.) The rabbinical canon of exegetical works, except for the Pesiqta, derives from the school. Out of the synagogue come three types of writings: first, a liturgy of prayers, found in the collective, anonymous *Siddur* and *Mahzor* for ordinary days and Days of Awe respectively; second, poetry written (and sometimes signed) by individuals and known as *piyyut*; and, third, translations of Scripture into Aramaic for popular utilization in the synagogue, called *Targumim.* We shall first survey how the topic of the Messiah is treated in writings which surely emerge from the synagogue, that is, the liturgy and the Targumim, then turn to those which reach us through the master-disciple-circle. My survey will be very brief and touch only on the main traits pertinent to our question. For liturgy and the Targumim, writings on which I have never worked, I merely summarize current scholarly results, as indicated.

II

The Messiah in the Synagogue Liturgy

In the Talmudic writings rabbis refer to the synagogue and its liturgy, in which they participate and the beliefs and petitions of which they wholly share.[3] But they tend to speak of prayer, in general, as something belonging to "them," that is, ordinary Jews, regarding the activities of the schools -- Torah learning, discipleship -- as an alternative, and superior, form of divine service. Accordingly, when we turn to the synagogue liturgy, the Siddur, we stand, if close to the rabbinical estate, essentially at the margins of that social entity. We cannot doubt that rabbis legislated the conduct of the prayer service. Both the Mishnah's laws and the Talmud's exegesis and expansion of them prove it. But we do not know who organized and arranged the prayers in the form which has come to us. References in the rabbinic canon to the service take for granted an established order of prayer, with which, in some minor details, rabbis too may tinker. But the givenness of the basic order of service, even in the references in the Mishnah, at the beginning of the rabbinic canon, suggest that the established mode of synagogue worship comes prior to rabbis' engagement with it. That is to say, the formation of the social group and literary document out of which Judaism as we know it took shape, intersects with other facts of an encompassing system, a Judaism in large measure concentric, but not totally symmetrical, with the rabbis' system. When, therefore, we find in the Siddur references to the coming of the Messiah, which express a larger construct of how history will come to an end and when Israel's destiny will reach fulfillment, we cannot be certain that rabbis framed and stood behind that construct. We know for certain only that all rabbis, in the centuries under study, affirmed and shared in that same set of convictions.

The Siddur, the order of the Judaic service, very simply is a messianic liturgy. Saturated through and through with the raw hope of the Jewish nation for the long-delayed Messiah, for a resolution of the this-worldly history of Israel, and for fulfillment of the redemption promised long ago, the Siddur fully expresses the Messiah myth as part of the larger, conventional eschatology. Wherever we look, at daily, sabbath, festivals, or holy day prayers, we find that same simple and compelling petition. There is no type of prayer, no occasion within the larger order of service, in which the Messiah in particular, or, at the very least, eschatological redemption in general, does not appear. True, at some

---

[3]Bibliography

Joseph Heinemann, *Prayer in the Talmud: Forms and Patterns* (Berlin and New York, 1977: Walter de Gruyter). Translated from the Hebrew by Richard S. Sarason.

Lawrence A. Hoffman, *The Canonization of the Synagogue Service* (Notre Dame and London, 1979: University of Notre Dame Press).

points, the Messiah myth may be bypassed in its definitive symbols, as in the *Qaddish*, repeated through the service. In the contemporary wording:

> Magnified and sanctified be his great name in the world which he hath created according to his will. May he establish his kingdom during your life and during your days, and during the life of all the house of Israel, even speedily and at a near time, and say ye, Amen. [Translated by S. Singer, *The Authorized Daily Prayer Book* (London, 1953, p. 37) and pass.][4]

But the rather general reference to "God's kingdom" does not end the matter. On the contrary, the Prayer, or so-called Eighteen Benedictions, does not speak only of gathering in the exiles and restoring Israel's own judges and counselors. There are two components, among the definitive number of nineteen, that make explicit reference to the coming of the Messiah. These deal, first, with the restoration of Jerusalem, then, with the advent of the Davidic monarch, and finally, with the rekindling of the fires on the altar of the Temple in Jerusalem (Singer, pp. 49, 50):

> And to Jerusalem, thy city, return in mercy, and dwell therein as thou hast spoken; rebuilt it soon in our days as an everlasting building, and speedily set up therein the throne of David. Blessed art thou, O Lord, who rebuildest Jerusalem.
>
> Speedily cause the offspring of David, thy servant, to flourish, and let his horn be exalted by thy salvation, because we wait for thy salvation all the day. Blessed art thou, O Lord, who causest the horn of salvation to flourish.
>
> Accept, O Lord our God, thy people Israel and their prayer; restore the service to the oracle of thy house; receive in love and favor both the fire offerings of Israel and their prayer; and may the service of thy people Israel be ever acceptable unto thee.
>
> And let our eyes behold thy return in mercy to Zion. Blessed art thou, O Lord, who restorest thy divine presence into Zion.

To give further instances, at the beginning of the new month, on the appearance of the New Moon, on the intermediate days of Passover and Tabernacles, in the grace after meals said on those days, we find further explicit references of the same character:

> Our God and God of our fathers! May our remembrance rise, come and be accepted before thee, with the remembrance of our fathers, of Messiah, the son of David, thy servant, of Jerusalem thy holy city, and

---

[4]I do not mean to suggest that the wording of the prayers before us necessarily goes back to the period under discussion. We do not know. But all authorities claim that the gist of the prayers was formalized by the end of late antiquity, if not long before, and on that basis I think it valid to proceed as we do.

of all thy people the house of Israel, bringing deliverance and well-being, grace, lovingkindness and mercy, life and peace on this day....

The equivalent Prayer for the New Year liturgy follows along these same lines (Singer, p. 239a):

Give then glory, O Lord, unto thy people, praise to them that fear thee, hope to them that seek thee, and free speech to them that wait for thee, joy to thy land, gladness to thy city, a flourishing horn unto David thy servant, and a clear shining light unto the son of Jesse, thine anointed, speedily in our days.

True, the theme of the Messiah's coming tends to serve in a subordinate position as part of the larger expression of hope for God's own rule. Nearly every explicit reference to the Messiah's coming occurs in a setting in which God's sole rule over the whole world forms the paramount petition. But the picture is clear and unambiguous. The cited passages form a small but representative corpus of evidence to show that, as I said, the liturgy of the synagogue constitutes a protracted plea for the coming of the Messiah.

To be sure, the wording in the formulations of the liturgy just reviewed derives from the liturgical canon framed long after the period under discussion. But the basic organization and arrangement of the prayers are generally regarded as the work of authorities prior to the formation of the rabbinical movement. Heinemann states the consensus:

"The basic structures and content of the [statutory] prayers, determined at that time [in the generation following the destruction of the Temple], have never since been altered, and to this very day constitute the essential components of the Jewish liturgy."[5]

He maintains that communal prayer received its order of topics toward the end of the period before 70.

"It seems reasonable to conclude that the Eighteen Benedictions antedate the destruction of the Temple by a considerable period of time."[6]

What testifies to the liturgy of the period is not the exact wording, but the fundamental themes of the Prayer. Hence we may assume with some confidence an early provenience for the explicit references to, and petitions for, the coming

---

[5](p. 13)

[6](p. 22)

of the Messiah. It follows that the basic characterization of synagogue liturgy stands firm. We deal with eschatological prayers framed mainly, though not solely, within the familiar messianic myth and symbols. Were we to encounter such people today as said those prayers with conviction then, we should imagine ourselves in a conventicle of messianists, awaiting the near-term cataclysm in human history.

The figure of the Messiah, the casting of the experience of worship around the coming redemption, and the framing of prayers to confront Israel's collective experience in history and politics do not speak in particular for the rabbinical group, who, we may imagine, concurred in the general sentiments at hand. In no way do the messianic statements constitute convictions distinctive to the rabbis' viewpoint. What is far more likely is that that group took for granted and made its own -- as it found useful and relevant -- an established viewpoint, which, of course, it shared anyway. The larger issue before us therefore is whether or not the liturgy contains marks of the rabbis' intervention. Did the rabbis reframe to their own measure the messianic symbol or the larger eschatological motif? The answer is that we discern not a trace of evidence of such a process. Whatever the wording, the fundamental topics remained fixed: restoration of Israel, Jerusalem, Zion, the Messiah; God's return to Zion; and reconstitution of the sacrificial cult. None of these was introduced by the rabbis. These powerful motives recur in daily and sabbath worship, on festivals and holy days, in the synagogue and in the grace after meals, and on virtually every other occasion for public prayers that one can imagine. The state of affairs taken for granted in the liturgy -- the destruction of Jerusalem and the end of the cult -- of course indicates that the liturgy in its final form reflects conditions after 70. But if the frame of mind of the survivors prevails, it is a persistent viewpoint, an ongoing and permanently appropriately petition.

III

The Messiah in the Targums

It is clearly a mistake to treat as a unitary corpus so varied a set of writings as *the* Targums[7] -- the Aramaic translations of Scripture generally assumed to have been read in the synagogue for the benefit of Jews who did not understand Hebrew.[8] One Targum, that bearing the name of Onqelos, cites passages from the Mishnah. So Targum Onqelos may be assumed to have been completed after

---

[7]My student, Paul Flesher, revised and corrected the account that follows.

[8]Bibliography

Michael L. Klein, *The Fragment Targums of the Pentateuch According to their Extant Sources* (Rome, 1980: Biblical Institute Press, Analecta Biblica, 76)

Samson H. Levey, *The Messiah: An Aramaic Interpretation. The Messianic Exegesis of the Targum* (Cincinnati, New York, Los Angeles, and Jerusalem, 1974: Hebrew Union College and the Jewish Institute of Religion).

Alexandro Diez Macho, *Neophyti 1* (Madrid and Barcelona, 6 vols., 1968-1977).

ca. A.D. 200 and to fall within the rabbinic framework. But we do not know that that Targum -- or any other -- constitutes a unitary document accomplished at essentially a single moment, and not the result of a process of collection and agglutination of ad hoc translations over a long period of time. We have no firm evidence about the dates of any of the other Targumim, or who may have done the translating, or why and for what particular audience or circumstance the work was undertaken.

True, we can show that certain facts (e.g., tales or details added to the Hebrew text by the Aramaic versions and taken for granted by translators of Scripture) were known early on. These details, then, must have circulated among some Jews at a fairly early time relative to the point at which a given Targum is first independently attested. It follows that Targums contain ideas from a time prior to their own closure and redaction[9]. But how those ideas took shape and came to expression in any given Targum is hardly clear. More important, the appearance of an idea otherwise attested at an early date does not constitute sufficient evidence that everything else in the Targum containing that early idea is equally early. All we know is that the translators, whenever they did their work, drew upon facts -- ideas, myths, motifs -- that circulated before their time. Knowing that later authors used earlier ideas presents no surprises and answers no questions. After all, we know as fact that all authors of Jewish writings in late antiquity cited ancient Scripture. But so what? What else do we know when we know that fact? In all, we enter a world of learning in which, beyond presentation of good versions of most of the documents, practically nothing has, as yet, been accomplished.

To ask about the place of the Messiah in the various Targums, we briefly review the panoply of symbols and images in which the Messiah myth is expressed, and look at the larger theory of Israel's history and destiny contained within that expression. In the extant evidence, however, the answers to our questions become difficult to evaluate. This is because we do not know whether rabbis in particular speak through any or all of the Targumim (apart from Onqelos) or whether rabbis represented in the canon of Mishnah, Talmud, and associated compilations of scriptural exegeses stand behind the translations. Since we cannot say when and where the documents came into being, we cannot know whose viewpoint they express or of which system they form a part. Still, Levey's collection does make possible a rapid survey and does permit some preliminary observations. However, we have to supplement our survey with two further editions of Targum texts, those of Diez Macho and M. Klein.

The first observation is that, for the Pentateuch, the several Targumim make little effort to introduce the theme of the Messiah at points where the text itself does not demand, or at least invite, it. We are reminded of the similar policy of

---

[9] That is the argument of Vermes and Bloch, discussed in Chapter Two.

Sifra and the two Sifrés.[10] Indeed, there are points without any allusion to the Messiah, where we might have expected the Messiah myth to make an appearance within the translators' exegesis of the Hebrew text. This includes, for instance, the prophecies, blessings and curses, of Leviticus 26-27 and Deuteronomy 28 and 32.

If we rapidly survey the several Targumim to the Pentateuch, what do we find? Let us begin with Onqelos, the most important for our purpose, and contrast what we find with the other Targumim. Onqelos's translation into Aramaic speaks of the Messiah in the following passages only (Levey, pp. 7, 21):

Gen. 49:10

The scepter shall not depart from Judah, nor the staff of law from between his feet until Shiloh comes. And unto him shall be the obedience of the peoples.

Onqelos

The transmission of dominion shall not cease from the house of Judah, nor the scribe from his children's children, forever, until the Messiah comes, to whom the Kingdom belongs, and whom nations shall obey.

Gen. 49:11

He binds his foal to the vine, his colt to the choice vine; he washes his garment in wine, and his robe in the blood of grapes.

Onqelos

He shall enclose Israel in his city, the people shall build his Temple, the righteous shall surround him, and those who serve the Torah by teaching shall be with him. His raiment shall be of goodly purple, and his garment of the finest brightly dyed wool.

Num. 24:17

I see him, but not now, I behold him but not near; a star shall step forth out of Jacob, and a scepter shall arise out of Israel, and shall crush the corners of Moab, and break down all the sons of Seth.

Onqelos

I see him, but not now; I behold him, but he is not near; when a king shall arise out of Jacob and be anointed the Messiah out of Israel. He shall slay the princes of Moab and reign over all mankind.

Num. 24:18

And Edom shall be an inheritance, and an inheritance, too, Seir, his enemies; but Israel shall do valiantly.

---

[10]I refer to my *Messiah in Context. Israel's History and Destiny in Formative Judaism* (Philadelphia, 1983: Fortress).

Onqelos

Edom shall become an inheritance and Seir shall become a possession of its enemies, but Israel shall prosper in wealth.

Since Targum Onqelos stands well within the rabbinic system, as I said, we are hardly surprised by the reference, along with the Messiah, to "those who serve the Torah by teaching." In the light of our survey of rabbinic compositions, to follow below, Onqelos' references prove sparing, indeed, nearly perfunctory. It is difficult to imagine how Gen. 49:10 can have been read as other than a messianic prediction. But then the substance is routine. The Messiah will rule and restore the Temple. Num. 24:17, with its reference to the "star out of Jacob," presents no surprises. The rest of the passage, which I have not cited, has Israel enjoy victory over its enemies, all of whom bear biblical names. So the repertoire of references is both limited and conventional. In this regard, Levey comments, "The main emphasis... is [on] the destruction of Rome, its utter annihilation down to the last man. The Messiah is a military figure performing relatively moderate deeds of valor, who becomes the ruler of the entire world" (p. 22).

The so-called "Palestinian" translations of the Pentateuch present a larger set of facts about the Messiah, but none of them can be shown to tell us what the rabbis, in particular, had in mind. Levey's collection of Pseudo-Jonathan and the Fragmentary Targum (hereinafter Psj and F) permits a rapid survey. We shall use Levey's translation of Psj, the translation of Targum Neofiti (hereinafter, TN) found in Diez Macho, and, following Klein's edition of the Fragmentary Targumim, we shall note the presence of messiah references in both ms. P and ms. V, but we shall quote only one text (Flesher contributed these latter references).

In the days of the King Messiah, the enmity between the serpent and woman will come to an end (Gen. 3:15, Psj, TN, P, V). The King Messiah will reveal himself at the tower of Eder (Gen. 35:21, Psj).

Gen. 49:1

And Jacob called to his sons and said, "Gather together, and I will relate to you what will happen to you at the end of days" (Levey, p. 5).

Psj

Then Jacob called his sons and said to them: "Purify yourselves of uncleanness, and I will tell you the hidden secrets, the concealed date of the End, the reward of the righteous and the punishment of the wicked, and what the pleasure of Paradise will be." The twelve sons of Israel gathered together around the golden bed on which he lay. As soon as the date of the End when the King Messiah would arrive was revealed to him, it was immediately concealed from him; and therefore, instead (of revealing the date) he said: "Come, and I will relate to you what will happen to you at the end of days" (Levey, p. 5).

F (ms. P)

And Jacob called his sons and he said to them: "Gather (also ms. V) together and I shall tell you what will befall you; the giving of reward to the righteous and the punishment that is destined to come upon the wicked, when they are all gather together in the end of days." They thought that he would reveal to them everything that is destined to come about in the final messianic period. However, after it was revealed unto him, it was concealed from him; and Jacob arose and blessed them, each according to his measure of [deserving] blessing did he bless them (Klein, 2:30).

TN

And Jacob called his sons and said to them: "Gather together and I will tell you the concealed secrets, the hidden ends, the giving of rewards of the just and the punishment of the wicked and what the happiness of Eden is." The twelve tribes gathered together and surrounded the bed of gold on which our father Jacob was lying after the end was revealed to him that the determined end of the blessing and the consolation be communicated to them. When the end was revealed to him the mystery was hidden from him. They hoped that he would relate to them the determined end of the redemption and the consolation. [But] when the mystery was revealed to him, it was hidden from him and when the door was open to him, it was closed from him. Our father Jacob answered and blessed them: each according to his good works he blessed them (Diez Macho, 1:633).

The conception that the time of the coming of the Messiah had been revealed and then forthwith concealed is familiar. The translators represented by Psj expand on the description of the King Messiah at Gen. 49:10. But they add no striking facts. The Fragmentary Targum combines the details of both Onqelos and Psj to the same passage, while TN elaborates upon the circumstances of the vision.

On the other hand, the Fragmentary Targums to Exod. 12:42 are truly formidable and original:

Exod. 12:42

It was a night of watching for the Lord, to bring them out of the land of Egypt. This same night for the Lord is one of watching for all the children of Israel throughout their generations (Levey, p. 12).

F (ms. V)

It is a night that is preserved and prepared for when the Israelites went forth redeemed from the land of Egypt. For four nights are written in the Book of Memories: The First night; when the memra of the Lord was revealed upon the world in order to create it; the world was unformed and void, and darkness was spread over the surface of the deep; and the memra of the Lord was light and illumination; and he called it the first night. The second night: when the memra of the Lord was revealed upon Abram between the pieces; Abram was one hundred years old, and Sarah was ninety years old; to fulfill that which Scripture says; "Behold, it is possible for Abram, at one hundred years, to beget [a child], and it is possible for Sarah at ninety years to give birth." Was not Isaac our father thirty-seven years old at the time that he was offered up upon the altar; the heavens bent low and descended; and Isaac saw their perfection, and his eyes were dimmed from [what he had beheld of] the heights; and he called it the second night. The third night: when the memra of the Lord was revealed upon the Egyptians in the middle of the night; his left hand was slaying the firstborn of the Egyptians; and his right hand was rescuing the firstborn of Israel; to fulfil that which Scripture says: "Israel is my firstborn son;" and he called it the third night. The fourth night: when the world will reach its fixed time to be redeemed; the evil-doers will be destroyed, and the iron yokes will be broken; and Moses will go forth from the midst of the wilderness and the King Messiah, from the midst of Rome: this one will lead at the head of the flock, and that one will lead at the head of the flock; and the memra of the Lord will be between both of them; and I and they will proceed together. This is the Passover night before the Lord; it is preserved and prepared for all the Israelites, through their generation (Klein, 2:126).

The substance of this passage, with its invocation of Moses as part of the eschatological drama, carries us far away from the ideas we have seen up to this point. Why thought about the Messiah should have taken this turn is not difficult to suggest, given the New Testament Gospels' identification of Jesus and Moses (see Levey, p. 13). So far as we know, the rabbinic canon does not resort to this same comparison. Hence the detail testifies to a theory of the Messiah of a system other than the rabbinic one. Accordingly, it serves a purpose to be investigated in a quite separate context from the present one.

Reference to anointing oil, Exod. 40:9-11, leads Psj to refer to the consecration of "the tabernacle and all that is in it for the crown of the kingdom of the house of Judah and the King Messiah, who is destined to redeem Israel at the end of days." Both fragmentary Targums add the actual prophecy of Eldad and Medad, Num. 11:26, which addresses Gog and Magog and their defeat by the King Messiah (Ezek. 39:9-10). When Psj reaches the prophecy of Balaam, Num. 24-17, the translation, unlike that of Onqelos, makes explicit reference to contemporary times, e.g., the Messiah's destruction of "the sinful city of Caesarea, the mighty city of the Gentiles." Here we recall the view that when Caesarea prospers, Jerusalem pines, and the contrary. But I see no direct connection. An example of the way in which Psj treats the matter is as follows, at Num. 24:24:

Troops ready for battle, with great armed might, shall go forth from Italy in Liburnian ships, joining the legions which shall go forth from Rome and Constantinople. They shall afflict the Assyrians and subjugate all the sons of Eber. However, the end of both these and those shall be to fall by the hand of the King Messiah and be destroyed forever.

Such an explicit reference to the Messiah's engagement in specific contemporary events is rare in the rabbinic canon. Levey comments (p. 24), "The Messianism is more drastic than that of [Onqelos]."

References to the Messiah in translations of Deuteronomy prove unexceptional. Deut. 25:19, "You must not forget," is expanded by Psj, "Even unto the days of the King Messiah, you shall not forget." Deut. 30:4, on gathering in the exiles, is referred to the messianic time: "He shall bring you back by the hand of the King Messiah." That does not seem a far-fetched expectation, within the established framework. But Elijah is included in context. So while the Messiah stands for the critical figure in eschatological time, he does not work alone. There is no detailed account of his person and origin.

What conclusions are we to draw? I really do not know, since, to me, all of these statements come out of no clear context whatsoever. On the one side, it is clear that Onqelos, the translation within the setting of the rabbinic system, proves reticent to introduce the Messiah at all. What Targum Onqelos does say falls entirely within the range of familiar details. But that does not prove "the rabbis" were in any way reticent to express a hope for the Messiah. The materials collected in the Babylonian Talmud surely prove the opposite. There were diverse rabbis' opinions, but the final redactors of the document left no doubt about their views. The different Palestinian Targums cover a wider variety of details. But the basic tendency of reticence on messianic themes characterizes these Targums as much as Onqelos. Where the text of Scripture does not absolutely demand a messianic exegesis, e.g., by referring to the end of days or some other eschatological notion, the authorities behind the various Palestinian Targums are not much more likely to introduce the figure of the Messiah than are those behind Onqelos. The contrast to the exegesis of the Pentateuch revealed in writings of the Church fathers, with their persistent interest in introducing the messianic dimension in every imaginable detail, hardly requires extensive illustration.

That fact tells us two things, neither of which is surprising.

First, the Christian exegetes find the exegetical fulcrum of all scriptural statements at the verses' relevance to the figure of Christ, the Messiah. What else should we have expected?

Then, second, the rabbinic and other Jewish exegetes have something else on their mind, at many points, than the figure of the Messiah in particular. What is that other point of insistence?

For both the more and the less rabbinic of the translations, it is the history of Israel, the Jewish people, and the labor of the Messiah in behalf of Israel in the eschatological conclusion to history. The larger systemic framework, in which both the Targum of Onqelos and the other Targumim find their appropriate location, is Israel's history and destiny. But how the specific assertions about the Messiah, and references to Israel's history and destiny encompassed within those assertions, serve the larger interests of a particular and distinctive system -- "a kind of Judaism -- I cannot say. As we see in Levey's summary, the main emphases of both Targumim, the Onqelos and the Pseudo-!! Jonathan, prove entirely consistent with the main outlines of messianic doctrine revealed in the rabbinic canon we shall survey below. Having relied so heavily on Levey, I let his summary conclude this discussion (pp. 31-32, parentheses mine):

> Targum Onqelos is most sparing in its messianic exegesis, and has messianic references only to Gen. 49:10-12 and Num. 24:17-20, 23-24.
>
> The Messiah is portrayed as a symbol of security, culture and refinement in Genesis, and in Numbers as a leader who will restore the political and military strength of Israel by gaining dominion over the entire world after he utterly destroys Rome. Jerusalem and its inhabitants will enjoy divine protection, represented by a rebuilt sanctuary. The social order will be undergirded by peace, prosperity, and righteousness, all under the influence of Torah which will become the universal law, and by the ideal of education, which will become a universal reality. Since O is composite, differing views are to be expected, here and there.
>
> Targum Pseudo-Jonathan has messianic references in its interpretations to Gen. 3:15; 35:21; 49:1, 10-12; Exod. 17:16; 40:9-11; Num. 23:21; 24:17-20, 23-24; Deut. 25:19; 30:4-9.
>
> The Messianism in Psj is not at all consistent. For example, in Num. 24:17 it is the Messiah who will vanquish Gog; in Exod. 40:11 this is to be achieved by the Ephraimite Messiah. In Deut. 30:4 the ingathering of the exiles is to be effected both by Elijah and by the Messiah. Psj dips into the messianic much more readily and freely than O, and he interprets as his fancy strikes him. Yet, considering the vast amount of Scriptural resources, he does not have an overabundance of messianic references.
>
> The picture of the Messiah as portrayed by Psj embraces all the features found in O, and a number of others besides. The Messiah son of Ephraim is introduced, something which is not found in the Messianism of the official Targumim, whether to the Pentateuch or to the Prophets. The vindication of Israel and the destruction of its enemies will be accomplished by a blood-bath, performed by the Messiah, who as the aggressive war-lord of the future, will himself be covered with the blood of the slain foe. Notwithstanding this, the era which he inaugurates will mark the end of war, the establishment of peace, justice and righteousness. The dispersed Jews will be gathered in, established once again on their own land, and will be purified by the elimination of the evil impulse and thereby will attain eternal life. This idea is tied with the Torah and ethic, and hinges on the performance of the commandments. Psj also discourages speculation as to the date of the advent of the Messiah.
>
> The Fragmentary Targum (mss. P&V) contains messianic interpretation in Gen. 3:15; 49:1 (ms. P only), 10-12 (ms. P vs 10 only, ms. V vss. 10-12); Exod. 12:42; Num. 11:26; 24:7, 17-20, 23-24.

The Messianism of F is essentially the same as that both of O and Psj, with several added features. F draws a comparison between Moses and the Messiah. He has the Messiah coming from Rome, not Palestine. He interprets the prophecy of Eldad and Medad as messianic prophecy. Targum Neofiti follows that other Palestinian Targum when it mentions the Messiah, but it refers to the Messiah in only one passage not found in TO, Gen. 3:15. The other passages are Gen. 49:10-12, Num. 24:17-20 and 23-24. The messianic exegesis found in Genesis is similar to that of Psj, whereas that in Numbers resembles the passages in the Fragmentary Targums.

The obvious question raised by this survey is this: What, if anything, is distinctive to the canon of formative Judaism as against that which is shared in common with the antecedent heritage of Israel, in general, and with non-rabbinic Jews of contemporary times? To this matter we now turn.

IV

The Rabbinical Context

Conceptions of the Messiah and doctrines of Israel's history and destiny certainly are not scattered at random across the entire corpus of canonical rabbinic writings. They fall into clear cut groups. Documents that contain one distinct set of facts stand apart from those that contain another. Many, though not all, of the symbols and myths a document does utilize turn out to play a significant part in expressing the fundamental viewpoint of the document in which they occur. The principle of selection is not random. On the contrary, we discern clear configurations of meaning that emerge from a given set of messianic symbols and myths revealed in a given document.

This is assuredly the case with the Mishnah. What its philosophers say about the Messiah turns out to be fully congruent with what they say about a great many other subjects. In a curiously convoluted way, the same is true also for the Talmud of Babylonia. But the purpose is different. We can scarcely point to a significant idea from some other, probably earlier, document, that we do not find in the Babylonian Talmud. If the compilers of that immense work had left an editors' manifesto, stating their intention to provide a compendium of opinions, a summa of Judaism, we should not be surpised. For that is precisely what they have given us. Yet, even here, among the masses of data they assemble, some facts play a substantial part, while others do not. The former serve larger doctrinal purposes, contribute to a more considerable argument, and make commonly invoked propositions in their own particular terms. Other facts are preserved but hardly touched. They appear normally (though not invariably) in the names of isolated individuals, not as the consensus of sages. The ideas expressed scarcely undergo development. No effort goes into relating those ideas to any others, even for the purpose of harmonization.

So, in all, the Mishnah stands at one side, the Talmud of Babylonia at the other, both in date of formation and closure -- ca. A.D. 200 and 600, respectively -- and in character. The one expresses a single system. The other contains and encompasses a well composed worldview, while it does not make an effort to present only one set of ideas. The intermediate documents tend to group themselves around one or the other of the poles, as the following summary tables indicate. The Tosefta, Sifra, and the other so-called tannaitic midrashim (compositions of scriptural exegesis serving the Pentateuch and containing the names only of authorities who appear also in the Mishnah) and the Rabbah-compilations may be located around the Mishnah's pole. The Talmud of the Land of Israel and Pesiqta de R. Kahana tend to take a position around the Babylonian Talmud's pole (to speak anachronistically).

The chart that follows lists the principal facts -- viewpoints about the Messiah, convictions, and allusions to mythic conceptions -- in the documents of the rabbinic canon. The rough provenience of these facts, the documents in which they occur, is indicated. The important result is, as I just said, to show us that the Mishnah and its associated documents of amplification and exegesis present a small number of selected facts. The other half of the canon, the Talmud's half, presents nearly all of the facts at hand. What this result, as illustrated in the tables, means has now to be suggested.

First, we surely cannot conclude that the authors of the Mishnah's portion of the canon did not know, or did not accept the validity of, the facts they did not use. Second, we cannot claim that the messianic eschatology entered the rabbinic system and served as its teleology only when the amplification of the Mishnah had run its course late in the formation of Judaism. Third, it further does not prove that opinion among the rabbis who were responsible for these documents (let alone among Jews not within the rabbinical framework) shifted radically from the second century to the fourth or fifth. We cannot demonstrate any of these three propositions.

What, then, do we know? On the positive side, we may reach the following simple conclusions.

First, when constructing their systematic "Judaism" -- that is, the world-view and way of life for Israel presented in the Mishnah -- the philosophers of the Mishnah did not make use of the Messiah-myth in the construction of a teleology for their system. They found it possible to present a statement of goals for their projected life of Israel which was entirely separate from appeals to history and eschatology. Since they certainly knew, and even alluded to, long standing and widely held convictions on eschatological subjects, beginning with those in Scripture, the framers thereby testified that, knowing the larger repertoire, they made choices different from others before and after them. Their document accurately and ubiquitously expresses these choices, both affirmative and negative.

Second, the appearance of a messianic eschatology fully consonant with the larger characteristic of the rabbinic system -- its stress on the viewpoints and prooftexts of Scripture, its interest in what was happening to Israel, its focus upon the national-historical dimension of the life of the group -- indicates that the encompassing rabbinic system stands essentially autonomous of the prior, mishnaic system. True, what had gone before was absorbed and fully assimilated. But the rabbinic system, in part expressed in each of the non-mishnaic segments of the canon, and fully spelled out in all of them, is different in the aggregate from the Mishnaic system. It represents more, however, than a negative response to its predecessor.

The rabbinic system took over the fundamental convictions of the Mishnaic worldview about the importance of Israel's constructing for itself a life beyond time. The rabbinic system then transformed the Messiah myth in its totality into an essentially ahistorical force. If people wanted to reach the end of time, they had to rise above time, that is, history, and stand off at the side of great movements of political and military character. That is the message of the Messiah myth as it reaches full exposure in the rabbinic system of the two Talmuds. At its foundation this is precisely the message of the teleology *without* eschatology expressed by the Mishnah and its associated documents. Accordingly, we cannot claim that the rabbinic system in this regard constitutes a reaction against the mishnaic one. We must conclude, quite to the contrary, that in the Talmuds and their associated documents we see the restatement in classical-mythic form of the ontological convictions that had informed the minds of the second century philosophers. The new medium contained the old and enduring message: Israel must turn away from time and change, submit to whatever happens, so as to win for itself the only government worth having, that is, God's rule, accomplished through God's anointed agent, the Messiah. To state matters in unrefined terms, salvation depended upon sanctification, which therefore took precedence as the governing principle of the worldview and way of life commanded by the rabbis' Torah. It follows, of course, that the rabbis who stand behind the principles of messianic eschatology, worked out in the Talmuds, in fact continued on an absolutely straight line the fundamental convictions of the Mishnah.

We now turn to the summary table, which, as I indicated, shows us the provenience of diverse assertions concerning the Messiah in the canonical corpus. I list the topics in order of their appearance in my *Midrash in Context* (Philadelphia, 1984: Fortress). Then I indicate where they occur in the documents according to the sequence in which those documents reached closure. The important point, however, is not documentary sequence. We must not confuse an evident precedence of one compilation over another with the historical pattern in which a given fact appeared before some other. That claim has not been made here. It is indemonstrable and, further, it is quite beside the point I wish to make.

The Messiah[*]

1. Messiah = anointed priest...a, b, c, d, e
2. Messiah = son of David (Ruth, Boaz).....................a, d, e, f,h, i, j, k, l
3. This age vs. age of the Messiah...a, b, d, e, h
4. Tribulations before Messiah...a, d, f, g, h
5. Sages suffer before the end...a, f, h
6. David's dominion is eternal..c, h, i
7. David's son restores horn of Israel..c, h, i
8. Messiah's coming and resurrection of dead.............................c, h, i
9. David as a rabbi..c, h
10. Messiah's name: Menahem..c
11. Messiah from Bethlehem...c
12. Messiah born when Temple destroyed...c
13. Aqiba said Bar Kokhba was a Messiah...c
14. When Israel repents, they will be saved (no messianic reference) ....c, h
15. Israel must be humble to bring Messiah. Bar Kokhba was arrogant and no messiah, so he lost ....c, h
16. Israel punished for neglect of Torah...c
17. If Israel would do..., the Messiah would come.......................c, d, h
18. Because Israel does..., the Messiah has not come.........................h
19. Messiah: David-Hillel...e
20. Messiah will gather exiles...e, h, i
21. Israel will not require the Messiah as teacher...............................e
22. Messiah records peoples' good deeds.......................................e, h
23. Unusual incidents prior to Messiah...f, h
24. Messiah comes to worst generation.......................................f, g, h
25. Messiah will come when God chooses, do nothing in advance ....f, h
26. Reckoning the end...f, h, k, l
27. Gentiles convert when Messiah comes..g
28. Gentile rule ends...g, h
29. God clothes Messiah..g
30. Description of person of the Messiah...g, h
31. God restores Jerusalem, Zion, Temple cult, through the Messiah ....g, h, i, j
32. 6000 years, Messiah's age the middle 2,000..............................g, h
33. Messiah came in Hezekiah's time. (Denied.)................................h
34. Messiah's name was Shiloh, etc..h
35. Length of Messiah's rule..h
36. Messiah in Nisan...g, h
37. Messiah in 7th year...h
38. Messiah not coming on a Sabbath..h
39. Prayer may bring the Messiah...h, i
40. Messiah comes in 468..h

[*]
a = Mishnah
b = Tosefta, Abot, and Abot de R. Nathan
c = Talmud of the Land of Israel
d = Mekhilta, Sifra, Sifre Num., Sifre Dt.
e = Gen. Rabbah and Lev. Rabbah
f = Lam. R., Est. R. I, Song R., Ruth R.

g = Pesiqta de R. Kahana
h = Talmud of Babylonia
i = Siddur
j = Targum Onqelos to the Pentateuch
k = Targum Pseudo-Jonathan to Pent.
l = Fragmentary Targum to the Pentateuch

Tracing the principal expressions of the Messiah myth across the canon of rabbinical writings tells us more about the canon than about the history of the Messiah myth. We see which documents tend to group themselves around a given set of ideas, and which stand essentially distinct from others. The Mishnah and its close associates, Abot, the Tosefta, and Abot der. Natan, fall together on the one end of the spectrum, while the Talmud of the Land of Israel and the Talmud of Babylonia fall on the other. Closer to the former pole are the exegetical compilations serving the Pentateuch, specifically, Mekhilta, Sifra, Sifré Numbers, and Sifré Deuteronomy (and some Targums). The Rabbah collections of the pre-Islamic period (Genesis Rabbah, Leviticus Rabbah, Lamentations, Song, Ruth, and Esther Rabbah I) fit somewhere closer to the pentateuchal-exegetical compilations than they do to either of the two Talmuds; and Pesiqta der. Kahana adjoins the Talmud of Babylonia.

We further see that the synagogue-based writings, both Siddur and Targum, form a group by themselves. We now realize that they treat the Messiah myth in an entirely different way. Concretely, they evoke the theme in all its mythic manifestations -- David, Jerusalem, Temple, cult, and the restoration of all of these -- but scarcely follow up with discussion of a single one of the propositions important in the scholastic compositions, e.g., factual statements and systemically consequential doctrines. The synagogue-writings -- Targumim, Siddur -- fit together and collectively stand apart from the rabbinical ones. That is the chief result at hand.

V

One Theme, Two Settings

Overall, therefore, we may group the rabbinical canon in (two parts and the entire corpus of Judaic writing from late antiquity into (at least) three: the Mishnah and its circle, on one side; the two Talmuds and their associates in the center; and outside of the circle of these schools, the synagogal compositions.[12]

---

[12]Once more we note that other writings produced by Jews, such as the Hekhalot, Sefer Hayesirah, and the like, appear to derive from still other life-situations than the synagogue or the school. But I do not know what these might have been.

Of these three, there can be no doubt about the principal and single most comprehensive document: the Talmud of Babylonia covers almost everything found in all the other writings. It is the great vacuum cleaner of ancient Judaism, sucking up the entire antecedent corpus. The achievement of its compilers, as is now clear, was to create encyclopedic summaries of all the data at their disposal, then to attempt, with only limited success to be sure, to harmonize the mass of contradiction and conflict which resulted.

VI

The Messiah and the Talmuds

The two components of the great rabbinical canon, the Mishnah and its friends, the two Talmuds and their associates, stand essentially separate from one another, though they are related in important ways. They are separate in that the Mishnah's circle covers a very limited number of topics and does so in a quite distinctive way. The Talmuds' circle covers the mishnaic material but encompasses a very much larger territory of its own as well. The Mishnah's circle exhibits its own traits of mind and method, presenting a system unto itself. The two Talmuds fully cover the Mishnah's range in their own way, absorbing the Mishnah's entire repertoire of ideas, one by one, but making those ideas, taken up discretely, into something quite other than what they had been when they were viewed as a whole.

The principal result of this survey is to uncover, for the subject at hand, two concentric circles. Were we to treat all documents as one harmonious statement of Judaism, we should have missed the distinction at hand. And it is a distinction that does make a difference. For the two circles of documents contain two "Judaisms," so to speak -- one small, the other huge, one quite compact and internally coherent, the other, while not totally formless, also not entirely self-consistent. Specifically, the Mishnah presents us with a complete system. The Talmuds offer us a huge repertoire of facts, a fair number of which serve as major elements in the system, while others remain unintegrated and discrete. As we have seen time and again, the Mishnah integrates everything that comes its way or that it selects. The Talmud uses to its own advantage some of the components of the larger Messiah myth while preserving, but essentially neglecting, others.

If I had to specify the *systemically*-characteristic, even definitive, elements of the larger factual catalogues at hand, I should have no difficulty in pointing to what the Mishnah finds critical, namely, the few topics appearing in the Mishnah column of the catalogue (Nos. 1-5 on the list of facts about the Messiah given above). Indeed, what the Mishnah does not utilize is more interesting than what it does. The Mishnah's framers chose for their system five facts, three of them commonplaces and (once the subject comes up) unavoidable. These are, first, that the Messiah comes from the house of David; second, that there is a difference between the present age and the age of the Messiah; and, third, that there will be tribulations before the coming of the Messiah, for people in general, but especially for sages. These commonplaces (excluding the sages' special suffering), deriving from Scripture and well known to virtually every writer on the subject of the Messiah, are joined by one that is considerably different from what we find elsewhere. For the Mishnah's system, there is no such thing as *the* Messiah. What we find, rather, is the *classification* messiah. Into that classification as utilized in the Mishnah's system fall two kinds of messiahs: (1) priests anointed for office as specified in Mosaic law, e.g., for the Temple, for the army, and (2) another, eschatological kind. The former appear extensively and play a significant part in specified tractates. The Messiah in the other guise, the one familiar to everyone else, appears only as part of the undifferentiated background of accepted, but systemically neutral, facts.

In the Mishnah and closely associated documents, the Messiah thus receives no close attention; no problems take shape around the laws affecting him or his age. That is, no generative problematic emerges out of the topic of the Messiah around which a tractate, an intermediate unit of discourse, or even a single pericope might take shape. Obviously, the Mishnah's framers wished to reshape the issue into terms they found interesting, hence their special concern for the classification "Messiah-priest" and their special pleading about the special suffering of sages in the awful times prior to the Messiah's coming. These facts about the use and neglect of the Messiah myth point to a single conclusion. The philosophers of the Mishnah chose to talk about other things.

We need hardly belabor the fact that the rest of the rabbinical canon saw matters otherwise. Our table requires no substantial amplification. What we do not find in the Mishnah, we find everywhere else. The points of literary and canonical classification, emerging from the distribution of facts among two or more collections, yield no important insight. The development of the rabbinical theory of history and the theology of Israel's history within a mythic framework do not lie before us. What we do find are answers to two questions. First, which facts specifically serve the larger system and which ones simply occur at random in the documents? The answer to that question emerges from a larger theory about the character of the rabbinical system. Second, what was rabbinic in particular? That is to say, that theory, to begin with, has to explain the relationship between what was distinctive to the schools and what was part of the general heritage of the Jewish nation. Let us take up this matter, since the answer to our question is right on the surface.

VII

The Rabbi and the Synagogue

When our mishnaic and talmudic documents treat the structure of the liturgy, they take for granted that rabbis bore responsibility for the organization of the prayers and arranged them in accordance with their standard mode of thought (exegesis of pertinent verses of Scripture). Hence, we need not doubt that the liturgy speaks *for* the rabbinical estate. The use of the liturgy in synagogues beyond rabbinical influence cannot be demonstrated. But we need claim no more than that the liturgy served people in synagogues -- whether or not in all synagogues -- and so spoke out of a common national-religious heritage. When viewed this way, the prayers tell us what formed part of a generally accepted heritage of conviction about the Messiah and about Israel's history. That heritage, then, presents commonplaces about the Messiah's bringing God's rule and his restoring Israel's Land, its holy city, and holy place. What views do the pertinent canonical documents suggest rabbis held that others did not?

Distinctive to rabbis are two matters. First, they expressed in their particular way what were in fact generally held convictions. Second, some of their formulations constitute doctrines which were distinctive to their own estate. In the present context, we may point to the notion that Israel can hope for just government only when God rules. That belief, though stated in a way peculiar to rabbis, in fact expresses what must have been a widespread yearning. But the doctrine that, to prove worthy of God's rule, Israel must accept the dominion of Gentiles and must demonstrate its humility in order to make itself worthy, and that rabbis must provide the model for the way in which Israel at large must live derive from, and express, the larger system of the rabbinical canon. They do not stand upon a single continuum with the generally held beliefs of the nation at large. They mark the rabbinical canon as distinctive, different from the literary-theological heritage of the people in general (if, beyond Scripture, such a thing can be said to have existed at all). So they express part of what made the rabbi rabbinical.

Bearing in mind this distinction between what was part of the antecedent, universal heritage of Israel, and what emerged from the distinctive system of the rabbis, we may rapidly review our catalogue of topics. Those that I regard as falling into the two categories just defined are as follows:

Generally held elements of the Messiah myth (including biblically supplied			Facts particular to the rabbinical canon and expressing its distinctive conceptions		
1	11	33 (?)	5	19	40
2	20	34	9	21 (?)	43 (?)
3	23	35	12 (?)	22 (?)	44
4	24 (?)	38	13	25	48 (?)
5	26 (?)	41 (?)	14	31 (?)	49 (?)
6	27	42	15	32	
7	28 (?)	45	16	36 (?)	
8	29	46	17	37 (?)	
10 (?)	30	47 (?)	18	39 (?)	

Obviously, the range of uncertainty spreads over the whole. Were we able to consult sources beyond those at hand, moreover, we should find reason to treat as generally known (if not demonstrably believed) facts the broader and perhaps different range of conceptions from those listed here. But we all have beyond the writings of the schools are the writings of the synagogue.

When we ask about the canonical context of the Messiah that emerges from the formative centuries of Judaism as we know it, we nonetheless can point with some certainty to elements congruent with broader national convictions and also can point out some elements which are distinctive to the rabbinical system. Indeed, we may claim to distinguish, among the latter, two systems -- the Mishnaic and the Talmudic. We may point to that rather small set of facts deemed by the former to be systemically important, as distinct from the much larger set of facts (including the small set) utilized by the latter. Why can we not specify that all facts found in the Talmuds play some clear part in the articulation of the rabbinical system exposed therein? The reason is that the Talmuds make no attempt to frame a complete and exhaustive statement of their viewpoint but include everything relevant, while excluding the irrelevant and, finally, systematize the whole.

VIII
Conclusion

The figure of the Messiah serves diverse purposes, which are defined by the framers of the larger systems in which Messiah-materials find a place. We know that the authors of the Mishnah assigned an insubstantial role to the Messiah. But did the framers of the ultimate rabbinical system, in particular the great encyclopedists of the Talmud of Babylonia, simply open the gate to admit "the Messiah" at large? I think not. What we find in the Talmudic sector of the formative canon of Judaism is not merely an established, general conception of the Messiah, which now was invited to serve (as it had so well elsewhere) as the principal teleological justification of the rabbinical system. True, the Messiah enters. But he does so only on the rabbis' terms. So he is incorporated into the rabbinical realm through a process of assimilation and (from the viewpoint I think dominant among the Mishnah's philosophers) also of neutralization.

By reshaping the teleology of the Mishnaic system into an eschatological idiom -- indeed, by restating the eschatology in the established messianic myth -- the rabbis of the Talmud made over the Mishnah's system. But if the Mishnah was thus forced into that very grid of history and eschatology that it had been formulated to reject, the Mishnah's mode of being in turn drastically modified the Messiah myth. For the latter was recast into the philosophical mode of thought and stated as teleology of an eternally present sanctification which was attained by obedience to patterns of holiness laid out in the Torah. This grid is precisely the one that the framers of the Mishnah had defined. By no means may we conclude that what changed, in the end, was the Mishnah's system. Its modes of thought intact, its fundamental points of insistence about Israel's social policy reaffirmed, the Mishnah's system ended up wholly definitive for Judaism as it emerged in the canon at the end of its formative centuries, the "one whole Torah of Moses, our rabbi."

How so? The version of the Messiah myth incorporated into the rabbinic system through the Talmuds simply restates the obvious: Israel's sanctification is what governs. So if Israel will keep a single Sabbath (or two in succession), the Messiah will come. If Israel acts with arrogance in rejecting its divinely assigned condition, the Messiah will not come. Everything depends, then, upon the here-and-now of everyday life. The operative category is not salvation through what Israel does but God's sanctification of what Israel is. The fundamental convictions of the Mishnah's framers, flowing from the reaction against the apocalyptic and messianic wars of the late first and early second centuries, here absorbed and redirected precisely those explosive energies that, to begin with, had made Israel's salvation through history the critical concern. So while the Talmuds introduced a formerly neglected myth, their version of the Messiah became precisely what the sages of the Mishnah and their continuators in the Talmud most needed: a rabbi-Messiah, who would save an Israel sanctified through Torah. Salvation then depends upon sanctification and is subordinated to it. To state the obvious, the Siddur contains no hint of all this.

The Mishnah then, proposed to build an Israelite worldview and way of life that ignored the immediate apocalyptic and historical terrors of the age. The Mishnah's heirs and continuators, who produced the other sector of the formative canon, did two things. They preserved that original policy for Israelite society. But they also accommodated an ongoing social and psychological reality: the presence of terror, the foreboding of doom, and Israel's ironclad faith in the God who saves. Israel remained the old Israel of history, suffering, and hope. The Mishnah's fantasy of an Israel beyond time, an Israel living in nature and supernature, faded away. It was implausible. The facts of history contradicted it. Yet Israel's condition, moral and social, must govern Israel's destiny -- in accordance with the Torah's rules, but also precisely as biblical prophecy and Mishnaic doctrine had claimed. What then could Israel do about its own condition? How could Israel confront the unending apocalypse of its own history? Israel could do absolutely nothing. But Israel could be -- become -- holy. That is why history was relegated to insignificance. Humble acceptance of the harsh rule of gentiles would render Israel worthy of God's sudden intervention, the institution of God's rule through King-Messiah.

Let us close by reverting to the two questions with which we opened. *If a category does not differentiate, then we ask what happens if we do differentiate. If it does differentiate, we ask what happens if we do not.*

If we read all of the sources within the category of *Judaism*, to which all writings, undifferentiated by any criteria, contribute facts, we should have missed the distinctions that we have now proved able to draw. Not only have these distinctions made their point, they also make a considerable difference. Why? Because we have also been able to relate the distinctive use of facts of the

Mishnah on the theme, the Messiah, to the larger systemic traits of the Mishnah and its theology. So too the interests of the two Talmuds in the theme at hand correlate with larger traits of mind exhibited in those documents over all. So what seems to me a valid exercise in testing the use of the category, *Judaism*, along with the category, *the Messiah*, that is, *the Messiah-idea in Judaism*, produces a striking and one-sided result. When we harmonize, we obscure, and when we differentiate, we clarify. By the criteria of the test announced at the outset, we conclude that no such thing as *Judaism*. Consequently, pictures of *the Messiah-idea in Judaism* distort and misrepresent diverse documents and their views on the subject. So the category-formation that yields both *Judaism* and *Messianism* proves profoundly flawed. We have now to ask about a better way of forming our categories.

Chapter Four

Systems and Their Contents:
Canon as Inductive Category

I
Category Formation and the Canon
A Preliminary Statement

An inductive approach to category-formation requires that we take up the pieces of evidence one by one and, to find out what they mean, propose by sorting out those data along lines they themselves dictate. But an inductive approach presents us with its own circularity. How shall I know what data to select for organization in categories if to begin with I do not know what data I wish to organize and categorize? So knowing what I have to form into categories tells me the principles of category-formation. But if I already know what data demand categorization, then do I not already have my categories? That circularity confronts us first of all. My problem is to point to an initial and generative category external to the data. Lacking such a principle of selection and organization outside of the data I propose to describe, analyze, and interpret, I find myself at that same impasse at which I have located others.

To restate matters as clearly as I can: [1] we can know nothing without categories that permit classification, yielding the possibility of describing facts, analyzing them, and interpreting them. [2] We wish to generate those categories out of the data themselves, rather than imposing categories external to the data, that is, we seek an inductive, rather than deductive, principle of category-formation. But [3] how do we know what data we wish to categorize and classify, if not throug!. some principle of category-formation that tells us one set of data belongs within the system, another set outside? So that is the circularity from which I have now to seek to emerge.

Let us stipulate at the outset that all data -- all forms of evidence, in writing, in stones, in material culture, in reference in all writings -- pertaining to people regarded as Jews, and no data associated with people not regarded as Jews, to begin with require categorization for purposes of description, analysis, and interpretation. But how, then, to begin the work of differentiation, if so external a category as just now specified tells me more merely that (1) *everything in* is in and (2) *everything out* is out? Better the dreaded circularity with which we began. My responsibility, then, is to propose a category external to the data and yet appropriate to them.

I find that generative principle for category-formation in the matter of the diverse institutional media by which the data are mediated from antiquity to the present. I refer to the differentiation among data imposed by the simple fact that some materials come to us in one medium,, some in another. Some reach us through the mediation of the diverse Christian churches. Some come to us through the continuous process of tradition of the Judaic religious institution, the synagogue, and its associated, and continuing institutions, e.g., the master-disciple circle, the school, and the like. Some data come to us by the happy accident of being preserved in the earth and dug up. These facts of transmission differentiate. How so? The third group of data -- that produced by archaeology -- bears no relationship to the first or the second, since, by definition, no one knew about it until it was dug up. It forms a single group. The materials preserved by, respectively, church and synagogue scarcely overlap. The former constitute one distinct group, the latter, another. And, further, that latter group -- the writings preserved by the synagogue -- constitutes not a library but a canon. That is to say, the synagogue preserved the writings of late antiquity, where and when it did, because the group that kept the materials and copied them and handed them on and treasured them regarded them as holy, a statement of God's will to Israel: Torah. So that set of data stands quite distinct from the other two. Consequently, I claim an objective set of facts, external to the character and quality of the data, and yet enormously consequential in making differentiations among the data.

Accordingly, some data come to us through the enduring institutions of the West, the synagogue and the church. Some data come to us accidentally, through survival in caves. Some data come to us in the form of writing, some data come to us in the form of surviving buildings, artifacts, and other evidences of material culture. The one set differs from the other, and that in the merely adventitious sense just now specified: medium of preservation and transmission. What is preserved and transmitted by people falls into one gross category, what is preserved and transmitted by accident of nature falls into another. And the people who did the preserving break up into distinct and scarcely intersecting groups as well. Precisely what comes down to us from the Jews of late antiquity and how does it reach us? As is clear, the answer to the second question covers both: we have evidence in two media, material artifacts of archaeological provenience and writings of various kinds. The former then form one category, the latter another. As to the latter, the media for the preservation of documents -- deliberate or accidental -- once more supply us with our criterion for differentiation. What Judaism in its later history preserved as holy -- that is, the canon of Judaism from late antiquity to the present -- we must treat as distinct from what others than Jews preserved. The distinction derives from circumstance and from without. So we can indeed generate differentiating categories, variables that derive from the data themselves. Do these distinctions make a difference? For reasons already suggested, it makes a difference to know that (some) outsiders found materials worth saving. And, along these same lines and critical to the argument: it also makes a difference to know that (some) Jews found materials worth saving.[1] Some writings of Jews reach us through the medium of the copyists of the churches, others through the serendipity of preservation in dry caves. Some books come down to us only through the medium of the synagogue. And those for that -- adventitious -- reason form one distinct corpus of data -- for reasons of a nearly-physical, and essentially material character.

So, in my judgment, the simplest category at hand is how -- by what medium -- materials reached us. The items that come to us through institutions under Jewish auspices, therefore from the synagogue, fall together into one group, and that is because of traits of all of these items and none of the others. I speak of course, of what later on became known as the Torah, that is, the canon of the Judaism that defined and preserved these books as a canon (not, for example, as a library). The other data find their points of cogency elsewhere; they do not form our problem here. And, to proceed, once the books that for clear and distinct reasons fall together into a group define the broadest perimeters of our category, the mode of subdividing that encompassing category also is defined. From the canon, we divide by the same principle of category-formation as has led to the recognition of the canon as the principal category, namely, by the books that make up the canon. These categories then find definition in the books that the canon for its part preserved one by one (not as part of an undifferentiated mass) -- and so on down to the very sentences.

So I claim to move from the mass of evidence, delimited in a gross and completely external way, to the formation of categories that we recognize on inductive and external grounds. That is to say, on the basis of a descriptive and external approach to the diverse data that Jews of late antiquity produced, we locate a direct road to the categories formed by the canon and its components. These then define and constitute the categories, and so, I claim, the principle of category-formation derives from an inductive examination of the entire corpus of evidence, divided to begin with only among the media by which the evidence was preserved and transmitted to us, divided at the second level by the criteria themselves dictated by media internal to the first of the subdivisions of the data we chose to take up: the canon of that Judaism that preserved and handed on these books and not other books. And so the process proceeds.

---

[1] We do not know whether or not Jews thought so too, since we have these writings only from institutions under Christian auspices. If there were groups of Jews who cherished these books and also saved them, they did not succeed in handing on their holy books to the present generation.

II

Challenges to the Canonical Principle of Category-Formation

Now in consequence of the theory at hand, we begin by describing, analyzing, and interpreting the documents, not ideas held in a variety of documents. Our category derives not from *Judaism* but from *Torah*, that is, canon. But when we take up as our generative category a single book or document deriving from Jews of ancient times, without making theological judgments about whether the authors were "loyal" or "normative" or "authentic," we do something genuinely new. It is not only new, it also is a secular approach. When we take up not a whole canonical, or official, literature but only a single book or document, and further, when we avoid judgments about normative or authentic or classical Judaism as against the heterodox or heretical kind, we set aside theological issues. Rather, we address descriptive and anthropological ones. That approach to the study of ancient Jewish writings still surprises believers of one kind or another.

When, furthermore, we approach the canon of that form of Judaism that did emerge as normative from late antiquity and did define the outlines of the history of the Judaism that was normative from the seventh to the nineteenth century, we commit a still more remarkable act. For, if some concede that all Jewish texts do not attest to a single Judaism, few grasp that to begin with we cannot treat as unified and harmonious all the texts preserved by rabbis from antiquity to the present time, that is, the canon, or, in common language, "rabbinic" or "Canon of Judaism in late antiquity" or simply "Judaism." Our work is to test, not to affirm at the outset, the premise that all books of the official canon of rabbinic Judaism form a single whole and harmonious "Torah." That fundamental dogma of the faith demands demonstration through the evidence itself. And the test must be a simple one. It is a test of description, analysis, and interpretation of the documents of the canon of Judaism, read, first, one by one, then, second, as connected to one another, and, third and finally as part of a single and harmonious system, a Judaism, thus, as a continuity. That test begins with my work and stands at its elementary stages even now. So, to return to the main point, when we take up a single book or document in the canon of Judaism as we know it, or in the canon of any other Judaism, and when we propose to describe, analyze, and interpret that book in particular, we violate the lines of order and system that have characterized earlier studies of these same documents. Not only so, but we open our question in a quite different way from earlier efforts to describe matters such as doctrine or belief. How so?

Until now canonical texts as testimonies to a single system and structure, that is, as I said, not to "*a Judaism*" or to a component of some larger Judaism, but to it, that is, to "*Judaism*." What sort of testimonies texts provide of course varies according to the interests of the scholars, students, and saints who study them. Scholars look for meanings of words and phrases or better versions of a text. For them, all canonical documents serve equally well as a treasury of philological facts and variant readings. Student look for the sense of words and phrases and follow a given phrase hither and yon as their teachers direct their treasure hunt. Saints study all texts equally, looking for God's will and finding testimonies to God in each component of the canon, in the case of Judaism, in each component of "the one whole Torah of Moses, our rabbi." And that is how it should be, for students, scholars, and saints within Judaism.

Among none of these circles, however, will the discrete description, analysis, and interpretation of a single text make sense. Why not? Because for them all texts ordinarily form a single statement in common, "Torah" in the mythic setting, "Judaism" in the philosophical and theological one. From that perspective people correctly expect each document to make its contribution to the whole, to the Judaism. If, therefore, we wish to know what "Judaism" or "the Torah" teaches on any subject, we simply open all the books equally. We draw freely on sayings relevant to that subject wherever they occur in the entire canon of Judaism. Guided only by the taste and judgment of the great "sages of the Torah" or, in formally-secular circumstances, orthodox professors at seminaries or ethnic-nationalist ones at universities, as they have addressed the question at hand, we do not merely describe "Judaism," we also declare dogma.

Composites of sayings on a single topic (in our example, "the Messiah") drawn from diverse books in no way violate the frontiers and boundaries that distinguish one part of the canon from some other part of the same canon. Why not? The theological conviction defines the approach. Frontiers and boundaries stand only at the outer limits of the whole Torah of Moses our rabbi. Within the bounds, "there is neither earlier nor later," that is to say, temporal (therefore all other differentiating) considerations do not apply. If temporal distinctions make no difference, no others do either. For people who want to study in an inductive way the formation of Judaism in late antiquity as well as the setting in which Christianity took shape, however, the analysis of the literary evidence of the Jewish canon requires a different approach from the received orthodox-scholarly one.

III

Describing a System Whole:

The Canonical Principle in Category-Formation

The limns of documents then generate, form, and define our initial system of categories. That is, the document to begin with is what demands description, then analysis by comparison and contrast to other documents, then interpretation as part of the whole canon of which it forms a part.[2] Now to the rules of description.

---

[2] I hasten to add, I do not take the canon to be a timeless category, as my analysis of the Mishnah and its associates indicates. Quite to the contrary, the canon itself takes shape in stages, and these form interesting categories for study.

Documents stand in three relationships to one another and to the system of which they form part, that is, to Judaism, as a whole. When we understand these relationships, we shall grasp not only the premise of this book, but the future of the study of Judaism in its formative centuries, therefore, also, of the study of the Christianity that took shape in the same context and circumstance.

Autonomy: Each document, it is clear, demands description, analysis, and interpretation, all by itself. Each must be viewed as autonomous of all others.

Connection: Each document also is to be examined for its relationships with other documents that fall into the same classification (whether that classification is simply "Jewish" or still more narrowly and hence usefully defined).

Continuity: Each document is to be allowed to take its place as part of the undifferentiated aggregation of documents that, all together, constitute the evidence of a Judaism, in the case of the rabbinic kind, the canon of the Torah.

How so?

Autonomy: If a document reaches us within its own framework as a complete book with a beginning, a middle, and an end, we do not commit an error in simple logic by reading that document as it has reached us, that is, as a book by itself.

Connection: If further a document contains materials shared verbatim or in substantial content with other documents of its classification, or if a document explicitly refers to some other writings and their contents, then we have to ask the question of connection. We have to seek the facts of connectedness and ask for the meaning of those connections.

Continuity: In the description of a Judaism, we have to take as our further task the description of the whole out of the undifferentiated testimony of all of its parts. For a Judaism does put together a set of once discrete documents and treat them as its canon. So in our setting we do want to know how a number of writings fit together into a single continuous and harmonious statement.

That is the point at which we do describe and analyze a Judaism. We therefore take up the task of interpreting that Judaism in the relationship between its contents and the context in which it makes its statement. In taking up the question of the harmony of the canon, whether of the rabbinic sources represented in this book by the Mishnah, or of the sources comprising the Pseudepigrapha, or of the writings of the Essenes of Qumran, or even of the Maccabean historians, we ask a theological question. And, in our context, that question elicits enormous interest: what after all was the Judaism of the Maccabean historians, or of the Essenes of Qumran, or of the authorship represented by Mark, or by the Mishnah?

By seeing the several components of the canons of the Judaisms of antiquity in sequence, first one by one, then one after the other in an orderly progression and sequence, and, finally, all together all at once, we may trace the histories of

Judaisms. We may see a given document come into being on its own, in its context and circumstance. So we interpret the document at its site.

Since many documents relate to others prior to themselves or are brought into relationship to later writings, the issue of connectedness and connection demands attention. And, finally, all together and all at once, a given set of documents does form a whole, a canon, a frame that transcends the parts and imparts proportion, meaning, and harmony to the parts -- a Judaism.

What do I hope to accomplish in the accurate description, to begin with through categories of its own devising, of a Judaism? The answer derives from the work on systemic analysis of Mary Douglas. Her stress is upon the conception that, "each tribe actively construes its particular universe in the course of an internal dialogue about law and order."[3] So, she says,

> Particular meanings are parts of larger ones, and these refer ultimately to a whole, in which all the available knowledge is related. But the largest whole into which all minor meanings fit can only be a metaphysical scheme. This itself has to be traced to the particular way of life which is realized within it and which generates the meanings. In the end, all meanings are social meanings.[4]

If I seek to state the large issues of that culture precisely as they are expressed through minute details of the way of life of those who stand within its frame, I have to start with the correct categories that encompass all the extant data of the culture at hand. These interrelate and define a coherent system. So at stake in category-formation is systemic description.

For once we have discerned the system which the compositors and framers of the books at hand evidently meant to create, we have the task before us of comparing that system to other systems, yielded both by Judaisms in their various stages and by other religious and cultural systems, in quite different contexts. For a system described but not juxtaposed to, and compared with, other systems has not yet been interpreted. Until we realize what people might have done, we are not going to grasp the things they did do. We shall be unable to interpret the choices people have made until we contemplate the choices they rejected. And, as is clear, it is the work of comparison which makes that perspective possible. But how do we compare systems?[5] In fact, whenever we try to make sense for ourselves of what alien people do, we are engaged in a work of comparison, that is, an experiment of analogies. For we are trying to make sense specifically by comparing what we know and do to what the other,

---

[3] Mary Douglas, *Implicit Meanings: Essays in Anthropology*, (London: Routledge & Kegan Paul, 1975), p. 5.

[4] p. 8.

[5] Much that is called 'comparative religions' compares nothing and is an exercise in the juxtaposition of incomparables. But it does not have to be that way.

the alien culture before us, seems to have known and to have done. For this purpose we seek analogies from the known to the unfamiliar. I am inclined to think the task is to encompass everything deemed important by some one group, to include within, and to exclude from, its holy book, its definitive text: a system and its exclusions, its stance in a taxonomy of systems. For, on the surface, what they put in they think essential, and what they omit they do not think important.

IV

Comparing Wholes
The Centrality of Redaction

Let me now spell out the foundations of the view that the work of category-formation should properly begin with the complete canon and work its way through documents and only then proceed to the components of two or more documents, e.g., their positions on one question or another, set side by side for contrast and analysis through comparison. Why so? Because the work of analysis rests upon establishing first the genus, and only then the species, and the comparison of one species of one genus with another species of a different genus proves parlous indeed. For when we do otherwise and deal with a species distinct from the genus which defines its traits and establishes the context of those traits, we do not really know what we have in hand. The context of a definitive trait not having been established, we cannot know the sense and meaning of a given detail, indeed, even whether the detail by itself defines and distinguishes the species of which it is a part. It is the genus which permits us to describe and analyze the species of that genus. When, therefore, we propose to undertake a work of comparison and contrast, we must begin at the level of the genus, and not at any lesser layer.

What that means is simple. The work of description, prior to analysis and so comparison and contrast, begins with the whole, and only then works its way down to the parts. The work of analysis, resting on such a labor of description, proceeds once more, as I have proposed, from the whole, the genus, to the parts, the species. Why do I maintain that the document defines the genus -- the document? The traits of the documents themselves decide the issue. They exhibit integrity, so that their contents in detail testify to the plan and program of the compositors of the compilations of exegeses of Scripture. Let me turn to the specific document that in an exemplary way validates this judgment.

V

The Argument of
The Integrity of Leviticus Rabbah

In my study of Leviticus Rabbah[6] I proposed to demonstrate in the case of that compilation of exegeses of Scripture that a rabbinic document constitutes a text, not merely a scrapbook or a random compilation of episodic materials. A text is a document with a purpose, one that exhibits the traits of the integrity of the parts to the whole and the fundamental autonomy of the whole from other texts. I showed that the document at hand therefore falls into the classification of a cogent composition, put together with purpose and intended as a whole and in the aggregate to bear a meaning and state a message. I therefore disproved the claim, for the case before us, that a rabbinic document serves merely as an anthology or miscellany or is to be compared only to a scrapbook, made up of this and that. In that exemplary instance I pointed to the improbability that a document has been brought together merely to join discrete and ready-made bits and pieces of episodic discourse. A document in the canon of Judaism thus does not merely define a context for the aggregation of such already completed and mutually distinct materials. Rather, I proved, that document constitutes a text. So at issue in my study of Leviticus Rabbah is what makes a text a text, that is, the textuality of a document. At stake is how we may know when a document constitutes a text and when it is merely an anthology or a scrapbook.

The importance of that issue for the correct method of forming categories -- the canonical principle, yielding categories defined by documents -- is clear. If we can show that a document is a mere miscellany, then traits of the document have no bearing on the contents of the document -- things that just happen to be preserved there, rather than somewhere else. Then the document cannot serve as a category for the organization of data into intelligible patterns. If, by contrast,

---

[6] *The Integrity of Leviticus Rabbah. The Problem of the Autonomy of a Rabbinic Document* (Chico, 1985: Scholars Press for Brown Judaic Studies). Note also *Comparative Midrash. The Plan and Program of Genesis Rabbah and Leviticus Rabbah* (Atlanta, 1986: Scholars Press for Brown Judaic Studies), which continues the foregoing. The problem of category-formation and the issue of the character of the corpus of rabbinic writing -- essentially unformed documents that serve equally and adventitiously to preserve and transmit "traditions," as is generally held, or essentially formed documents, each with its integrity and viewpoint, formal traits and substantive message, as I argue for Leviticus Rabbah, Genesis Rabbah, Sifra, the Yerushalmi, the Bavli, and the Mishnah -- proves critical here. The entire argument I present is a single statement, in a number of distinct parts. My effort to prove the integrity of the several components of the rabbinic canon takes the form of, first, a fresh translation with exegesis (ordinarily form-analytical exegesis), second, description of the document on its own, and, third, an effort to place the document in its canonical context and in its historical context. I cannot point to any systematic effort to demonstrate the harmonies of the documents, justifying citing anything from anywhere without differentiation or distinction in composing a picture of the whole. Everyone seems to take for granted facts that, in fact, have not been demonstrated and, in my judgment, are wrong. I should have to reprint the larger part of my resume's bibliography to guide the reader to my studies of the formal and substantive plan and program of nearly the whole of the rabbinic corpus, but a summary of one small part of the issue -- how the several principal documents constitute components of that one whole Torah of Moses our Rabbi -- is in my *The Oral Torah. The Sacred Books of Judaism. An Introduction* (San Francisco, 1985: Harper & Row).

the text possesses its own integrity, then everything in the text must first of all be interpreted in the context of the text, then in the context of the canon of which the text forms a constituent. It follows, on the basis of the character of the canonical writings, one by one, that each forms an autonomous unit, possessing its own integrity, presenting its own viewpoint and evidence in support of that viewpoint. All of its contents, therefore, have to attest, to begin with, to that context in which they reach us: the document at hand. Hence my stress on the description and comparison of whole documents rests upon the result of the study of Leviticus Rabbah.[7]

Two principal issues frame the case. The first is what makes a text a text. The textuality of a text concerns whether a given piece of writing hangs together and is to be read on its own The second is what makes a group of texts into a canon, a cogent statement all together. At issue is the relationship of two or more texts of a single, interrelated literature to the world-view and way of life of a religious tradition viewed whole.

Why do these issues prove urgent in a study of category-formation? Because of a possible claim by proponents of the view that *Judaism*, consequently also *Midrash*, and *Messianism* form valid categories without respect to the documents in which data happen to turn up. They may wish to argue that the character of the documents supports their view, not mine. How so? They point to the fact that stories and exegeses move from document to document. The travels of a given saying or story or exegesis of Scripture from one document to another validate comparing what travels quite apart from what stays home. So traveling materials enjoy their own integrity, apart from the texts that quite adventitiously give them a temporary home.

If that fact characterizes the bulk of the materials contained in a given document, then that document's integrity turns out to be quite beside the point. Since the materials are shared among a number of documents, the boundaries of the document at hand mark a distinction that makes no difference. We therefore may assemble materials without the slightest regard for their original point of origin or provenience. We may assemble and use sayings and stories within categories quite separate from those generated by the components of the canon. For example, all sayings and stories on God, Torah, or Israel may fall into those categories, and this without regard to the literary-canonical facts affecting the transmission of those sayings. These facts will have been shown to affect nothing, if the documents that comprise the canon form neutral vessels for whatever happens to turn up in them. The canon then is not the right category, but another -- such as Judaism -- may be. So the issue is critical to my argument. I settle it, for the document at hand, in the study of Leviticus Rabbah, and each of the components of the rabbinic canon will in due course

---

[7] I shall presently take up the problem of sayings and stories that occur in two or more documents and ask how these find a place in the larger theory of the literature I offer in this still broader conception of category-formation.

have to undergo equivalent study. The problem of *Integrity* therefore is whether or not a rabbinic document stands by itself or right at the outset forms a scarcely differentiated segment of a larger and uniform *tradition* -- not canon but tradition -- one made up of materials that travel hither and yon, everywhere in the canon, and take up residence indifferent to the traits of their temporary abode in a particular book.

Let us now consider the contrary view. The reason one might suppose that, in the case of the formative age of Judaism, a document does not exhibit integrity and is not autonomous is simple. The several writings of the rabbinic canon of late antiquity, formed from the Mishnah, ca. A.D. 200, through the Canon of Judaism in late antiquity of Babylonia, ca. A.D. 600, with numerous items in between, do share materials -- sayings, tales, protracted discussions. Some of these shared materials derive from explicitly-cited documents. For instance, passages of Scripture or of the Mishnah or of the Tosefta, cited verbatim, will find their way into the two Canon of Judaism in late antiquities. But sayings, stories, and sizable compositions not identified with a given, earlier text and exhibiting that text's distinctive traits will float from one document to the next.

That fact has so impressed students of the rabbinic canon as to produce a firm consensus of fifteen hundred years' standing. It is that one cannot legitimately study one document in isolation from others, describing its rhetorical, logical, literary, and conceptual traits and system all by themselves. To the contrary, all documents contribute to a common literature, or, more accurately, religion -- Judaism. In the investigation of matters of rhetoric, logic literature, and conception, whether of law or of theology, all writings join equally to given testimony to the whole. For the study of the formative history of Judaism, the issue transcends what appears to be the simple, merely literary question at hand: when is a text a text? In the larger context of that question we return to the issue of the peripatetic sayings, stories, and exegeses.

When I frame matters in terms of the problem of the rabbinic document, I therefore ask what defines a document as such, the text-ness, the textuality, of a text. How do we know that a given book in the canon of Judaism is something other than a scrapbook? The choices are clear.

One theory is that a document serves solely as a convenient repository of prior sayings and stories, available materials that will have served equally well (or poorly) wherever they took up their final location. In accord with that theory it is quite proper in ignorance of all questions of circumstance and documentary or canonical context to compare the exegesis of a verse of Scripture in one document with the exegesis of that verse of Scripture found in some other document.

The other theory is that a composition exhibits a viewpoint, a purpose of authorship distinctive to its framers or collectors and arrangers. Such a characteristic literary purpose -- by this other theory -- is so powerfully particular to one authorship that nearly everything at hand can be shown to have been (re)shaped for the ultimate purpose of the authorship at hand, that is, collectors and arrangers who demand the title of authors. In accord with this other theory context and circumstance form the prior condition of inquiry, the result, in exegetical terms, the contingent one.

To resort again to a less than felicitous neologism, I thus ask what signifies or defines the "document-ness" of a document and what makes a book a book. I therefore wonder whether there are specific texts in the canonical context of Judaism or whether all texts are merely contextual. In framing the question as I have, I of course lay forth the mode of answering it. . We have to confront a single rabbinic composition, and ask about its definitive traits and viewpoint.

But we have also to confront the issue of the traveling sayings, the sources upon which the redactors of a given document have drawn. By "sources" I mean simply passages in a given book that occur, also, in some other rabbinic book. Such sources -- by definition prior to the books in which they appear -- fall into the classification of materials general to two or more compositions and by definition not distinctive and particular to any one of them. The word "source" therefore serves as an analogy to convey the notion that two or more sets of authors have made use of a single, available item. About whether or not the shared item is prior to them both or borrowed by one from the other at this stage we cannot speculate.

As I said, these shared items, transcending two or more documents and even two or more complete systems or groups, if paramount and preponderant, would surely justify the claim that we may collect sayings from here and there to describe (a) Judaism, without attention to context. Why? Because there is no context defined by the limits of a given document and its characteristic plan and program. All the documents do is collect and arrange available materials. The document does not define the context of its contents. If that can be shown, then we may quite properly ignore the contextual dimension imparted to sayings, including exegeses of Scripture, by their occurrence in one document rather than some other.

Let me now summarize this phase of the argument. We ask about the textuality of a document -- is it a composition or a scrap book? -- so as to determine the appropriate foundations for category formation as well as the correct classifications for comparative study. We seek to determine the correct context of classification. My claim is simple: once we know what is unique to a document, we can investigate the traits that characterize all the document's unique and so definitive materials. We ask about whether the materials unique to a document also cohere, or whether they prove merely miscellaneous. If they do cohere, we may conclude that the framers of the document have followed a single plan and a program. That would in my view justify the claim that the framers carried out a labor not only of conglomeration, arrangement and selection, but also of genuine authorship or composition in the narrow and strict sense of the word. If so, the document emerges from authors, not merely arrangers and compositors. For the same purpose, therefore, we also take up and analyze the items shared between that document and some other or among several documents. We ask about the traits of those items, one by one and all in the aggregate. In these stages we may solve for the case at hand the problem of the rabbinic document: do we deal with a scrapbook or a cogent composition? A text or merely a literary expression, random and essentially promiscuous, of a larger theological context? That is the choice at hand.

Since we have reached a matter of fact, let me state the facts as they are. To begin with, I describe the relationships among the principal components of the literature with which we deal. The several documents that make up the canon of Judaism in late antiquity relate to one another in three important ways.

First, all of them refer to the same basic writing, the Hebrew Scriptures. Many of them draw upon the Mishnah and quote it. So the components of the canon join at their foundations, in the Scripture and the Mishnah.

Second, as the documents reached closure in sequence, the later authorship can be shown to have drawn upon earlier, completed documents. So the writings of the rabbis of the canon of Judaism in late antiquity corpus accumulate and build from layer to layer. But, as we realize, that hardly exhausts the claim of those who see all the books as one big book.

Third, as I have already hinted, among two or more documents some completed units of discourse, and many brief, discrete sayings, circulated, for instance, sentences or episodic homilies or fixed apothegms of various kinds. So in some (indeterminate) measure the several documents draw not only upon one another, as we can show, but also upon a common corpus of materials that might serve diverse editorial and redactional purposes.

The extent of this common corpus can never be fully known. We know only what we have, not what we do not have. So we cannot say what has been omitted, or whether sayings that occur in only one document derive from materials available to the editors or compilers of some or all other documents. That is something we never can know. We can describe only what is in our hands and interpret only the data before us. Of indeterminates and endless speculative possibilities we need take no account. In taking up documents one by one, do we not obscure their larger context and their points in common?

In fact, shared materials proved for Leviticus Rabbah not many and not definitive. They form an infinitesimal proportion of Genesis Rabbah, under 3-

5% of the volume of the *parashiyyot* for which I conducted probes.[8]. Materials that occur in both Leviticus Rabbah and some other document prove formally miscellany and share no single viewpoint or program; they are random and brief. What is unique to Leviticus Rabbah and exhibits that document's characteristic formal traits also predominates and bears the message of the whole. So much for the issue of the peripatetic exegesis. To date I have taken up the issue of homogeneity of "sources,"in a limited and mainly formal setting, for the matter of how sayings and stories travel episodically from one document to the next.[9] The real issue is not the traveling, but the unique, materials: the documents, and not what is shared among them. The variable -- what moves -- is subject to analysis only against the constant: the document itself.[10]

VI

The Integrity of a Document in the Canon of Judaism

To describe and analyze documents one by one violates the lines of order and system that have characterized all earlier studies of these same documents. But the hermeneutical issue dictated by the system -- hence, as I have argued, the canon and its components -- overall defines the result of description, analysis, and interpretation. Simple logic makes self-evident the proposition that, if a document comes down to us within its own framework, as a complete book with a beginning, middle, and end, in preserving that book, the canon presents us with a document on its own and not solely as part of a larger composition or construct. So we too see the document as it reaches us, that is, as autonomous.

If, second, a document contains materials shared verbatim or in substantial content with other documents of its classification, or if one document refers to the contents of other documents, then the several documents that clearly wish to engage in conversation with one another have to address one another. That is to say, we have to seek for the marks of connectedness, asking for the meaning of those connections. It is at this level of connectedness that we labor. For the purpose of comparison is to tell us what is like something else, what is unlike

---

[8] There were two kinds of exceptions. First, entire *parashiyyot* occur in both Leviticus Rabbah and, verbatim, in Pesiqta der. Kahana. Second, Genesis Rabbah and Leviticus Rabbah share sizable compositions. The former sort always conform to the formal program of Leviticus Rabbah. They in no way stand separate from the larger definitive and distinctive traits of the document. The latter sort fit quite comfortably, both formally and programmatically, into both Genesis Rabbah and Leviticus Rabbah, because those two documents themselves constitute species of a single genus, as I shall point out below.

[9] *The Peripatetic Saying. The Problem of the Thrice-Told Tale in Talmudic Literature* (Chico, 1985).

[10] I repeat that these results refer solely to the one document on which I have worked systematically. Only when the entire set of principal documents of the third, fourth, and fifth centuries have been analyzed with reference to materials they share among themselves (not only with the Mishnah, at the one end, and the Talmud of Babylonia, at the other) shall we have a clear picture of the facts of the matter. The contrary claim as presently formulated, that everything is everywhere, rests on no analysis known to me.

something else. To begin with, we can declare something unlike something else only if we know that it is like that other thing. Otherwise the original judgment bears no sense whatsoever. So, once more, canon defines context, or, in descriptive language, the first classification for comparative study is the document, brought into juxtaposition with, and contrast to, another document.

Finally, since the community of the faithful of Judaism, in all of the contemporary expressions of Judaism, concur that documents held to be authoritative constitute one whole, seamless "Torah," that is, a complete and exhaustive statement of God's will for Israel and humanity, we take as a further appropriate task, if one not to be done here, the description of the whole out of the undifferentiated testimony of all of its parts. These components in the theological context are viewed, as is clear, as equally authoritative for the composition of the whole: one, continuous system. In taking up such a question, we address a problem not of theology alone, though it is a correct theological conviction, but one of description, analysis, and interpretation of an entirely historical order.

In my view the various documents of the canon of Judaism produced in late antiquity demand a hermeneutic altogether different from the one of homogenization and harmonization, the ahistorical and anti-contextual one definitive for contemporary category-formation. As I showed in the opening unit of this chapter, it is one that does not harmonize but that differentiates. It is a hermeneutic shaped to teach us how to read the compilations of exegeses first of all one by one and in a particular context, and second, in comparison with one another.

VII

A Fond Adieu to "Judaism"

Let us conclude with the point with which we began, the difficulty attached to generating categories for the present purpose out of theological or philosophical concepts. Why *Torah*, a literary principle of category-formation, not *Judaism*, a theological one? To answer that question, we turn to the greatest work ever published in any language[11] under the title *Judaism*, namely, George Foot Moore, *Judaism. The Age of the Tannaim* (Cambridge, 1927: Harvard University Press). Here we shall gain access to the main problem with the category at hand. The critical problem of definition is presented by the organizing category, "Judaism." Moore does not think definition is needed. But we now know that it is. Explaining what we propose to define when we speak about "Judaism" is the work of both contemporary philosophy of religion and history of religion. Moore fails to tell us also of whom he wishes to speak. So

---

11 E. E. Urbach, *The Sages, Their Concepts and Beliefs* (Jerusalem, in Hebrew: 1969, English, 1975: The Magnes Press) provides much valuable information but lacks intellectual cogency. It has not enjoyed a favorable reception. I explain why presently.

his repertoire of sources for the description of "Judaism" in the "age of the Tannaim" is awry. He makes use of sources which speak of people assumed to have lived in the early centuries of the Common Era, even when said sources derive from a much later or a much earlier time. What generates this error is a mistake in category-formation.

Specifically, Moore had to confront the problem of dealing with a category asymmetrical to the evidence. An essentially philosophical construct, "Judaism," is imposed upon wildly diverse evidence deriving from many kinds of social groups and testifying to the state of mind and way of life of many sorts of Jews, who in their own day would scarcely have understood one another, for instance, Bar Kokhba and Josephus, or the teacher of righteousness and Aqiba. So for Moore "Judaism" is a problem of ideas, and the history of Judaism is the history of ideas abstracted from the groups that held them and from the social perspectives of said groups. This seems to me a fundamental error, making the category "Judaism" a construct of a wholly fantastic realm of thought: a fantasy, I mean. In this regard matters are admirably summed up in Arthur Darby Nock's inquiry about the matter of "Gnosticism." He wanted to know where are the Gnostic churches, who are the Gnostic priests, and what are the Gnostic church's books and doctrines.[12] What he meant was to point out that what we have are rather specific evidences of a single genus, the Gnostic one, e.g., of Manichaeism or Mandaism and now, of Nag Hammad; out of the agglutination and conglomeration of these diverse social groups and their writings scholars (not Jonas alone) formed (I should say invented) that higher idea, that "*the*" -- the Gnostic religion. That the forms the counterpart of the *ism*-izing of *Juda-ism*.

From a philosophical viewpoint the intellectual construct, Gnosticism, may bear scrutiny. From an historical viewpoint, it does not. The reason is that the -*ism* of *Gnostic-*, as much as the -*ism* of *Juda -*, *ism*-izes too quickly and facilely. That is to say, Moore and other systematic theologians who have studied *Judaism* join together into harmonies data that derive from quite diverse groups at different times,and that were produced and preserved under different circumstances. So little is proved and much assumed. If we propose to present a cogent picture of how data deliver a single message, then the harmony and unity of the data demand demonstration. Before we know that the data derive from a single category, we can hardly undertake to form those data into a cogent statement about that category, describing, e.g., its ideas, analyzing its positions in comparison to the positions of other, related groups, interpreting those ideas in a still larger context. None of these routine activities of intellect can begin without a clear demonstration that the *it* -- the -*ism* -- is an *it* to begin with, and not a *them*. History, rightly done, must err on the side of radical nominalism, as against the philosophical power for tolerance of something close to pure realism. In invoking these categories of medieval philosophy for analogical

---

[12] Arthur Darby Nock, *Essays on Religion and the Ancient World*, ed. Zeph Steward (Oxford, 1972: Clarendon Press), I, 444-51, in his review of Hans Jonas, The Gnostic Religion.

purposes, I mean only to explain why, for the present purpose, *"Juda"* + *"ism"* do not constitute self-evident, let alone definitive, categories. So, as I said, Judaism constitutes a category asymmetrical to the evidence adduced in its study. The category does not work because the principle of formation is philosophical and not historical. And to begin with historical category-formation, we start with the sources at hand: once more, the canon, or, in mythic terms, the Torah.

Second, Moore's work to begin with is not really a work in the history of religions at all -- in this instance, the developmental and formative history of a particular brand of Judaism. His research is in theology. It is organized in theological categories. This again derives from the faulty generative principle of category-formation. Moore presents a synthetic account of diverse materials, (deriving from diverse sources, as I said) focused upon a given topic of theological interest. Apart from the use of the past tense, e.g., in Urbach's case, *the sages said* or *the sages believed*, there is nothing even rhetorically historical in the picture of opinions on these topics, no pretense of systematically accounting for development and change. What is constructed as a static exercise in dogmatic theology, not an account of the history of religious ideas and -- still more urgent -- their unfolding in relationship to the society of the people who held those ideas. Moore in no way describes and interprets the religious world-view and way of life expressed, in part, through the ideas under study. He does not explore the interplay between that world-view and the historical and political context of the community envisioned by that construction of a world. So far as history attends to the material context of ideas and the class structure expressed by ideas and institutions alike, so far as ideas are deemed part of a larger social system and religious systems are held to be pertinent to the given political, social, and economic framework which contains them, Moore's account of dogmatic theology to begin with has nothing to do with religious history, that is the history of Judaism in the first two centuries of the Common Era. So much for *Judaism* and for the principle of category formation that yields *Judaism, Midrash, Messianism.*

Moore hardly presents the sole exercise in the description of not Torah or the Torah but "Judaism." Before concluding, we do well to examine the approaches of two others, currently in common circulation. The one is Ephraim Urbach, the other E. P. Sanders, the former deeply learned in the literature of the Torah, the latter possessed of thin and superficial knowledge, used for purposes extraneous to the literature at hand. Both present important proof that the received principles of category-formation, together with their consequent categories, distort the evidence and confuse all issues of description, analysis, and interpretation. Since both works have found a sizable reception, we do well to examine them in some detail. They prove that I do not elaborately disprove mere nonsense -- positions no one holds anyhow. The contrary is the case. Everyone describes Judaism, few imagine that we should describe, analyze, and interpret the Torah -- by the categories generated by the Torah.

Ephraim E. Urbach, professor of Talmud at the Hebrew University and author of numerous articles and books on the Talmud and later rabbinic literature, presents a compendious work[13] intended "to describe the concepts and beliefs of the Tannaim and Amoraim and to elucidate them against the background of their actual life and environment." When published in Hebrew, in 1969, the work enjoyed immediate success, going into a second edition within two years, reaching English in 1975 in a serviceable, if clumsy, translation. Urbach is an imposing figure in Israeli scholarly and religious-political circles, serving as president of the Israel Academy of Sciences and Humanities and running for the presidency of the State of Israel as candidate of the right-wing and "religious" political parties. Within Orthodox Judaism Urbach derives from the German stream, which proposes to combine piety with academic learning.

The work before us has been accurately described by M.D. Heer:

> "He [Urbach] outlines the views of the rabbis on the important theological issues such as creation, providence, and the nature of man. In this work Urbach synthesizes the voluminous literature on these subjects and presents the views of the talmudic authorities."[14]

The topics are as follows: belief in one God; the presence of God in the world; "nearness and distance -- Omnipresent and heaven;" the power of God; magic and miracle; the power of the divine name; the celestial retinue; creation; man; providence; written law and oral law; the commandments; acceptance of the yoke of the kingdom of heaven; sin, reward, punishment, suffering, etc.; the people of Israel and its sages, a chapter which encompasses the election of Israel, the status of the sages in the days of the Hasmoneans, Hillel, the regime of the sages after the destruction of the Temple, and so on; and redemption. The second volume contains footnotes, a fairly brief and highly selective bibliography, and alas, a merely perfunctory index. The several chapters, like the work as a whole, are organized systematically, consisting of sayings and stories relevant to the theme under discussion, together with Urbach's episodic observations and comments on them.

In the context of earlier work on talmudic theology and religion. Urbach's contribution is, as I said, a distinct improvement in every way. Compared to a similar, earlier compendium of talmudic sayings on theological subjects, A. Hyman's *Osar divre hakhamin ufitgamehem* (1934), a collection of sayings laid out alphabetically, according to catchword, Urbach's volumes have the advantage of supplying not merely sayings but cogent discussions of the various sayings and a more fluent, coherent presentation of them in essay form. Solomon

---

[13]*The Sages. Their Concepts and Beliefs* . By Ephraim E. Urbach. Translated from the Hebrew by Israel Abrahams. Jerusalem: The Magnes Press, The Hebrew University, 1975. Two volumes -- I. Text: pp. xxii and 692. II. Notes: pp. 383.

[14]*Encyclopaedia Judaica* 16:4

Schechter's *Some Aspects of Rabbinic Theology* (1909, based on essays in the *Jewish Quarterly Review* printed in 1894-1896) covers exactly what it says, some aspects, by contrast to the much more ambitious dimension of the present work.

The comparision to George Foot Moore's *Judaism* , considered just now, is somewhat more complex. Moore certainly has the advantage of elegant presentation. Urbach's prose, in I. Abraham's English translation, comes through as turgid and stodgy, while Moore's is the opposite. By contrast to Moore, Urbach introduces sayings of Amoraim into the discussion of each category, and since both Urbach and Moore aim to present a large selection of sayings on the several topics, Urbach's work is on the face of it a more comprehensive collection. Urbach's own comments on his predecessors (I, pp.5-18) underline the theological bias present in most, though not all, former studies. Wilhelm Bousset and Hugo Gressmann, *Die Religion des Judentums im spaethellenistischen Zeitalter* (1926) is wanting because rabbinic sources are used sparingly and not wholly accurately and because it relies on "external sources," meaning apocryphal literature and Hellenistic Jewish writings. Urbach's own criticism of Moore, that "he did not always go deeply enough into the essence of the problems that he discussed," certainly cannot be leveled against Urbach himself. His further reservation is that Moore "failed to give an account of the origin of the beliefs and concepts, of their struggles and evolution, of their entire chequered course till their crystallization, of the immense dynamism and vitality of the spiritual life of the Second Temple period, of the tension in the relations between the parties and sects and between the various sections of the Sages themselves." This view underlines the historical ambition of Urbach's approach and emphasizes his view of his own contribution, cited at the outset: to elucidate the concepts and beliefs of the Tannaim and Amoraim against the background of their actual life and environment. Since that is Urbach's fundamental claim, the work must be considered not only in the context of what has gone before, in which, as I said, it emerges as a substantial step forward, but also in the setting of its own definition and understanding of the historical task, its own theory of how talmudic materials are to be used for historical knowledge. In this regard it is not satisfactory.

There are some fairly obvious problems, on which we need not dwell at length. Urbach's selection of sources for analysis is both narrowly canonical and somewhat confusing. We often hear from Philo, but seldom from the Essene Library of Qumran, still more rarely from the diverse works assembled by R.H. Charles as *the apocrypha and pseudepigrapha of the Old Testament* , and the like. If we seek to describe the talmudic rabbis, surely we cannot ask Philo to testify to their opinions. If we listen to Philo, surely we ought to hear -- at least for the purpose of comparison and contrast -- from books written by Palestinian Jews of various kinds. That accounts for much of the confusion, since the canon is not defined and defended, only assumed. But what makes Philo canonical and the Targumim not canonical? Urbach does not say. In this respect Moore's work proves far better. The Targumim are allowed no place at all because they are deemed "late." Within a given chapter, the portrayal of the sources will move rapidly from biblical to Tannaitic to Amoraic sources, as though the line of development were single, unitary, and harmonious, and as though there were no intervening developments which shaped later conceptions. Differentiation among the stages of Tannaitic and Amoraic sayings tends to be episodic. Commonly, slight sustained effort is made to treat them in their several sequences, let alone to differentiate among schools and circles within a given period. Urbach takes with utmost seriousness his title, the sages, their concepts and beliefs, and his "history," topic by topic, reveals remarkably little variation, development, or even movement. It would not be fair to Urbach to suggest that all he has done is publish his card-files. But I think his skill at organization and arrangement of materials tends to outrun his interest in differentiation and comparison within and among them, let alone in the larger, sequential history of major ideas and their growth and coherent development over the centuries. One looks in vain for Urbach's effort to justify treating "the sages" as essentially a coherent and timeless group.

Let us turn, rather, to the more fundamental difficulties presented by the work, because, as I said, it is to be received as the definitve and (probably) final product of a long-established approach to the study of talmudic religion and history. Urbach has certainly brought to their ultimate realization the methods and concepts of his predecessors. That is why I invoke Urbach's work as an example of the flaws and failures of established modes of category-formation.[15] For, above all, this is a work of categories -- theological ones.

First, let us ask, does the world-view of the talmudic sages emerge in a way which the ancient sages themselves would have recognized? From the viewpoint of their organization and description of reality, their world-view, it is certain that the sages would have organized their card-files quite differently. We know that is the case because we do not have, among the chapters before us, a single one which focuses upon the theme of one of the orders, let alone tractates, within which the rabbis divided and presented their various statements on reality, e.g., Seeds, the material basis of life; Seasons, the organization and differentiation of time; Women, the status of the individual; Damages, the conduct of civil life including government; Holy Things, the material service of God; and Purities, the immaterial base of divine reality in this world. The matter concerns not merely the superficial problem of organizing vast quantities of data. The talmudic rabbis left a large and exceedingly complex, well-integrated legacy of

---

[15]I am not certain whether, and how extensively, Sanders, dealt with presently, used Urbach in the Hebrew, since Sanders' book came out before the English translation of Urbach's. But Urbach surely takes priority over Sanders as exemplar of the category, *Judaism*. Sanders is not really interested in Judaism at all.

law. Clearly, it is through that legacy that they intended to make their fundamental statements upon the organization and meaning of reality. An account of their concepts and beliefs which ignores nearly the whole of the halakhah surely is slightly awry.

In fairness to Urbach, I must stress that he shows himself well-aware of the centrality of halakhah in the expression of the world-view of the talmudic rabbis. He correctly criticizes his predecessors for neglecting the subject and observes,

> "The Halakha does not openly concern itself with beliefs and concepts; it determines, in practice, the way in which one should walk... Nevertheless beliefs and concepts lie at the core of many Halakhot; only their detection requires exhaustive study of the history of the Halakha combined with care to avoid fanciful conjectures and unfounded explanations."

Urbach occasionally does introduce halakhic materials. But, as is clear, the fundamental structure of his account of talmudic theology is formed in accord not with the equivalent structure of the Talmud -- the halakhah -- but with the topics and organizing rubrics treated by all nineteenth and twentieth-century Protestant historical studies of theology: God, ethics, revelation, and the like. That those studies are never far from mind is illustrated by Urbach's extensive discussion of whether talmudic ethics was theonomous or autonomous (I, pp. 320ff.), an issue important only from the viewpoint of nineteenth-century Jewish ethical thought and its response to Kant. But Urbach's discussion on that matter is completely persuasive, stating what is certainly the last word on the subject. He can hardly be blamed for criticizing widely-held and wrong opinions.

Second, has Urbach taken account of methodological issues important in the study of the literary and historical character of the sources? In particular, does he deal with the fundamental questions of how these particular sources are to be used for historical purposes? The answer is a qualified negative. On many specific points, he contributes sporadic philological observations, interesting opinions and judgments as to the lateness of one saying as against the antiquity of another, subjective opinions on what is more representative or reliable than something else. If these opinions are not systematic and if they reveal no uniform criterion, sustainedly applied to all sources, they nonetheless derive from a mind of immense learning. Not all judgment must be critical, and not all expression of personal taste systematic. The dogmatic opinions of a man of such self-evident mastery of the tradition, one who, in addition, clearly is an exemplar of the tradition for his own setting, are important evidence for the study and interpretation of the tradition itself, particulary in its modern phase.

Yet we must ask, if a saying is assigned to an ancient authority, how do we know that he really said it? If a story is told, how do we know that the events the story purports to describe actually took place? And if not, just what are we to make of said story and saying for historical purposes? Further, if we have a saying attributed to a first-century authority in a document generally believed to have been redacted five hundred or a thousand years later, how do we know that the attribution of the saying is valid, and that the saying informs us of the state of opinion in the first century, not only in the sixth or eleventh in which it was written down and obviously believed true and authoritative? Do we still hold, as an axiom of historical scholarship, *ein muqdam umeuhar* ["temporal considerations do not apply"] -- in the Talmud?! And again, do not the sayings assigned to a first-century authority, redacted in documents deriving from the early third century, possess greater credibility than those first appearing in documents redacted in the fifth, tenth, or even fifteenth centuries? Should we not, on the face of it, distinguish between more and less reliable materials? The well-known tendency of medieval writers to put their opinions into the mouths of the ancients, as in the case of the Zohar, surely warns us to be cautious about using documents redacted, even formulated, five hundred or a thousand or more years after the events of which they speak. Urbach ignores all of these questions and the work of those who ask them.

There is yet a further, equally simple problem. The corpus of evidence is simply huge. Selectivity characterizes even the most thorough and compendious accounts, and I cannot imagine one more comprehensive than Urbach's. But should we not devise means for the filtering downward of some fundamental, widely- and well-attested opinions, out of the mass of evidence, rather than capriciously selecting what we like and find interesting? We have few really comprehensive accounts of the history of a single idea or concept. Urbach himself has produced some of the better studies which we do have. It seems somewhat premature to describe so vast a world in the absence of a far more substantial corpus of *Vorstudien* of specific ideas and the men who held them than is available. Inevitably, one must characterize Urbach's treatment of one topic after another as unhistorical and superficial, and this is despite the author's impressive efforts to do history and to do it thoroughly and in depth. He is not merely selective. He is downright capricious. And that seems to me decisive proof of the importance of correct and articulated principles of category-formation. We simply do not know why and how Urbach has chosen the topics he has selected, or what told him what evidence belonged, and what did not, in the articulation of these topcis. It is all a mystery, accounting, perhaps, for the vehement defense the work has received overall. Heat takes the place of light, as usual.

After all, Urbach has done this great work without the advantage of studies of the history of the traditions assigned over the centuries to one authority or another. He has at hand scarcely any critical work comparing various versions of a story appearing in succesive compilations. He has no possibility of recourse to comprehensive inquiries into the Talmud's forms and literary traits, redactional tendencies, even definitive accounts of the date of the redaction of most of the literature used for historical purposes. He cannot consult work on the thought of any of the individual Amoraim or on the traits of schools and circles among them, for there is none of critical substance. Most collections which pass as biographies even of Tannaim effect no differentiation among layers and strata of the stories and sayings, let alone attempting to describe the history of the traditions on the basis of which historical biography is be recovered. The laws assigned, even in The Mishnah-Tosefta, to a given Tanna have not been investigated as to their underlying presuppositions and unifying convictions, even their gross thematic agendum. If Urbach speaks of "the rabbis" and differentiates only episodically among the layers and divisions of sayings, in accord either with differing opinions on a given question or with the historical development of evidently uniformly-held opinions, he is no better than anyone else. The episodic contributions he himself makes in large measure constitute such history of ideas as presently is in hand. And, as I said, even that history is remarkable for the pre-critical methods and uncritical presuppositions upon which it is based.

Nor have I alluded to the intractable problems of internal, philosophico-theological analysis of ideas and their inner structures, once their evident historical, or sequential, development, among various circles and schools of a given generation and over a period of hundreds of years, has been elucidated. That quite separate investigation and analysis of the logic and meaning of the concepts and beliefs of the sages requires definition in its own terms, not in accord with the limited and simple criteria of working historians. If Urbach does not attempt it, no one else has entirely succeeded either. In this regard, Urbach's cavalier dismissal of the work of Marmorstein, Heschel, and Kadushin, among others, present us with a case of pure quackery. I doubt Urbach grasps the problems that Heschel and Kadushin proposed to solve. So he announces his purely subjective evaluations. While they may not have "persuaded" Urbach of the correctness of their theses, while they may have been wrong in some of their conclusions, and while their methods may have been unrefined, they at least have attempted the task which Urbach refuses even to undertake. One of the less fortunate aspects of Urbach's book, which makes for unpleasant reading, is the way in which he treats the work of other scholars. In the case of the above-named, this is not only disgraceful, it also is disastrous for Urbach's own undertaking. And since the whole opinion on works of considerable scholarship is the single word "worthless" or "unpersuasive," it may be observed that there is certain subjectivity which seems to preclude Urbach's reasoned discussion of what he likes and does not like in the work of many others and to prevent any sort of rational exchange of ideas. That is what I mean by quackery.

Urbach's work, as I said, in the balance brings to their full realization the methods and suppositions of the past hundred years. I cannot imagine that anyone again will want, from these perspectives, to approach the task of describing all of "the concepts and beliefs of the Tannaim and Amoraim," of elucidating all of them "against the background of their actual life and environment." So far as the work can be done in accord with established methods, here it has been done very competently indeed. Accordingly, we may well forgive the learned author for the sustained homiletical character of his inquiry and its blatantly apologetic purposes:

> The aim of our work is to give an epitome of the beliefs and concepts of the Sages as the history of a struggle to instill religious and ethical ideals into the everyday life of the community and the individual, while preserving at the same time the integrity and unity of the nation and directing its way in this world as a preparation for another world that is wholly perfect... Their eyes and their hearts were turned Heavenward, yet one type was not to be found among them... namely the mystic who seeks to liberate himself from his ego and in doing so is preoccupied with himself alone. They saw their mission in work here in the world below. There were Sages who inclined to extremism in their thoughts and deeds, and there were those who preached the way of compromise, which they did not, however, determine on the basis of convenience. Some were severe and exacting, while others demonstrated an extreme love of humanity and altruism. The vast majority of them recognized the complexities of life with its travail and joy, its happiness and tragedy, and this life served them also as a touchstone for their beliefs and concepts.

All of this may well be so, but it remains to be demonstrated as historical fact in the way in which contemporary critical historians generally demonstrate matters of fact. It requires analysis and argument in the undogmatic and unapologetic spirit characteristic of contemporary studies in the history of ideas and of religions. But in the context in which these words of Urbach are written, among the people who will read them, this statement of purpose puts forth a noble ideal, one which might well be emulated by the "sages" -- exemplars and politicians of Orthodox Judaism -- to whom, I believe, Urbach speaks most directly and persuasively, and by whom (alone) his results certainly will be taken as historical fact. The publishing success of the book and the recognition accorded its learned author are hopeful signs that the ideal of the sage of old indeed has not been lost upon their most recent avatars. It is by no means a reduction of learning to its sociological and political relevance to say that, if it were only for his advocacy of the humane and constructive position just now quoted. Urbach has made a truly formidable contribution to the contemporary theological life of Orthodox Judaism.

To respond to a work of such importance as Urbach's, it will not suffice to outline what is wrong with his book. Having stressed, for example, the importance of beginning the inquiry into the world-view of the talmudic rabbis with the study of the law, in particular of the earliest stratum, faithfully represented by the Mishnah with the Tosefta, I have now to propose the sorts of work to be done. Since I have raised the question of how we know what is assigned to a person was really said by him, and since by implication I have suggested that we cannot affirmatively answer that question, what sort of inquiry do I conceive to be possible, and upon what historical-epistemological basis? Let me here present very briefly an alternative conception of how to define and approach the formidable task accomplished by Urbach in accord with the prevailing methods and within established suppositions about the detailed and concrete historicity of talmudic evidences: the description of the world-view of "our sages." What happens when Fundamentalism dies, as it will even in Orthodox Jerusalem?

The problems that lie ahead and the line of research leading to their solution are now to be specified. Let us begin with the matter generally regarded as settled: the meaning of the texts. While philological research by Semitists and archaeological discoveries self-evidently will clarify the meanings of words and the identification of objects mentioned in the rabbinical literature, there is yet another task, the fresh exegesis of the whole of rabbinical literature within the discipline of contemporary hermeneutical conceptions. The established exegesis takes for granted an axiom which is simply false: that all texts are to be interpreted in the light of all other texts. Talmudic discussion of the Mishnah and its meanings invariably shapes the received interpretation of the Mishnah, for example. If Tosefta -- itself a commentary -- supplies a conception of the Mishnah's principle or rule, then Tosefta places the imprint of its interpretation upon the meaning of the Mishnah.

Now no one would imagine that the original meaning of Tanakh is regularly to be uncovered in the pages of Midrash or in the medieval commentaries to the Scriptures. On the contrary, everyone understands that Tanakh has been subjected to a long history of interpretation, and that history, while interesting, is germane to the original meaning of Tanakh only when, on objective and critical grounds, we are able to affirm it by historical criteria. By contrast, discussion of Mishnaic pericopae in Talmud and medieval commentaries and codes invariably exhausts the analysis of the meaning of Mishnaic pericopae. It is to the credit of H. Albeck (a better scholar than Urbach) that his excellent commentary to The Mishnah makes the effort at many points deliberately to exclude considerations introduced only later on. This is done not merely to facilitate a simple and popular interpretation, though Albeck admirably succeeds in doing just that, but also to present what Albeck considers to be the primary and original meaning of the law. It is no criticism of Albeck, limited as he was by his form, a commentary of the most abbreviated sort, to say that the discussion of the primary meaning of the Mishnah has to begin.

What is meant is simply, What did these words convey to the people who made them up, in the late first and second century? What issues can have been in their minds? True, much is to be learned from the answers to these questions supplied by the exegetes from the third to the twentieth century. But since, in the main, the supposition of the established exegetical tradition is non-historical and therefore uninterested in what pericopae meant at the outset, the established tradition, without re-evaluation, will not serve any longer. That is not to suggest it cannot be drawn upon. The contrary is the case. I know no other road into the heart of a pericope. At the same time, the established agendum -- the set of issues, problems, and questions deemed worth consideration -- is to be drastically reshaped, even while much that we have received will be reaffirmed, if on grounds quite different from those which motivated the great exegetes.

The classical exegetes faced the task of showing the profound interrelationships, in logic and meaning, of one law to the next, developing and expanding the subtleties and complexities of law, in the supposition that in hand is a timeless and harmonious, wholly integrated and unitary structure of law and logic. In other words, the established exegetical tradition properly and correctly ignores questions of beginnings and development, regarding these questions as irrelevant to the true meaning of the law under the aspect of eternity. And that is indeed the case -- except when we claim to speak about specific, historical personalities, at some one time, who spoke the language of their own day and addressed the issues of their own epoch. Urbach claims to tell us not about "talmudic Judaism" in general -- organized, as is clear, around various specific topics -- but to describe the history and development of talmudic Judaism. Yet, if that is the case, then the sources adduced in evidence have to be examined with the question in mind, What did the person who made up or formulated this saying mean to tell us? And the answer to that question is not to be located either by repeating the essentially eisegetical results already in hand, or by pretending that everything is obvious.

We have to distinguish between the primary issue, present to begin with in a pericope, and secondary problems or considerations only later on attached to the pericope. How do we confidently distinguish between the primary message of a pericope and the secondary eisegesis found in the great commentaries? We have to ask, What does the narrator, legislator, or redactor propose to tell us in a particular, distinct pericope? That is to say, through the routine form-analytical and literary-critical techniques already available, we have to isolate the smallest units of tradition, and, removing them from their redactional as well as their exegetical-eisegetical framework, ask about their meaning and original intent. Modes of emphasis and stress, for example, are readily discerned. Important materials will commonly be placed at the beginning of a pericope, or underlined through balanced, contrary allegations. But stylistic considerations and formal traits are helpful primarily in isolating pericopae and establishing their primary units for analysis. What is decisive is the discernment of what the narrator includes or omits, what seem to be his obvious concerns and what he ignores.

Once the importance of a fresh exegesis of rabbinical texts is established, the next problem is to select the documents on which the work should begin. The issue of category-formation recurs. Which documents? All of them together? One by one? On what basis do we choose? Here Urbach's work illustrates the fateful error of assuming that rabbinical literature is essentially timeless, so that there is "neither early nor late in Torah." Applied to the present work, it results in the notion that whatever is attributed to anyone was really said by the person to whom the saying is attributed, therefore tells us about the period in which he lived -- and this without regard to the date at which the document in which the said saying occurs was redacted, as I have stressed. Thus side by side in Urbach's compilation are sayings in the Mishnah and in late Amoraic and even medieval compilations of materials. In a fresh approach to the problem of the history of talmudic Judaism, we should, I believe, establish guidelines by which we evaluate materials first occurring in late compilations. The Mishnah-Tosefta assuredly comes to redaction by ca. A.D. 200. On the face of it, The Mishnah-Tosefta therefore constitutes a more reliable testimony to the mind of second-century rabbis than does *Yalqut Shimeoni* or *Yalqut Reuveni*. If that is obvious, then it follows that we have to begin our work with the analysis of the main ideas attributed to authorities in the Mishnah and the Tosefta. These have clearly to be worked out, and the materials occurring in later compilations, of Amoraic and medieval origin, are to be tested for conceptual and even thematic congruence against the materials occurring in earlier documents.

A further descriptive historical task is to be undertaken. When we concentrate attention on the most reliable witnesses to the mind of the earlier rabbis, those of the first and second century, we find ourselves engaged primarily in the analysis of legal texts. The Mishnah-Tosefta and related literature focus attention on halakhic problems. Are there underlying unities of conception or definitions of fundamental principles to be discerned within the halakhah? No one familiar with the literature and its classical exegesis is in doubt that there are. These are to be spelled out with some care, also correlated and compared to conceptions revealed in writings of other Jews, not solely rabbinic Jews, as well as Christians and "pagans." When, for example, we describe primary concerns and perennial issues inherent in laws attributed to Ushans, we find that, in much acute detail, rather fundamental issues of physics are worked out, e.g., the nature of mixtures, which will not have surprised Stoic, natural philosophers. Again, an enduring interest of Yavnean pericopae is in the relationship between intention and action, an issue both of interest to Paul and those who told stories about Jesus, on the one side, and of concern to philosophers of disaster and rebuilding in the earlier destruction, for instance, Jeremiah. The thought of Yavneh in any event has to be brought into relationship with the context in which the rabbis did their work, the aftermath of the loss of the Temple, just as the work of the Ushans, following the much greater this-worldly catastrophe brought on by Bar Kokhba, must always be seen against the background of crisis. Indeed, the formation of earlier rabbinic Judaism, from its primitive beginnings after 70 to its full and complete expression by the end of Ushan times in 170, is the product of an age of many painful events, events deemed at the time to bear the most profound theological weight. Much of the halakhah both can and should be interpreted in this particular context, and many of its issues, not to be reduced to economic or social concerns, express profound thought on the issues and inner meanings of the age itself. It follows that once the exegetical work is complete (if provisionally) and the historical sequences of individual units of law fairly well established, the larger issues emergent in underlying unities of conception and definitions of fundamental principles are to be uncovered, so that the legal materials may produce a history of major ideas and themes, not merely sets of two or three logical-temporal sequences of minor details.

In time we shall see the outlines of the much larger history of legal, therefore religious, ideas, the unfolding of the world-view of the rabbis who created rabbinic Judaism. These outlines will emerge not merely from discrete sayings, chosen more or less at random, about topics of interest chiefly to us, e.g., was rabbinical ethics theonomous or autonomous? what did "the rabbis" believe about life after death, the Messiah, eschaton? and so on. Rather, the morphology of the rabbinic world-view will emerge inductively, differentiated as to its historical stages and as to the distinctive viewpoints and conceptions held by individual authorities or circles within which that larger world-view originated. A new approach to the description and interpretation of the world-view of the earlier rabbis should emerge. This proceeds along critical-historical lines, taking account of the problems of dating sayings, of the diversity of the documents which purport to preserve opinions of the earlier masters, and the like. That is important, to be sure. But there are more important aspects of this work.

People do not seem to realize the immense dimensions of the evidence in our hands. We have much more than just a few sayings on this and that. We have a vast law-code, a huge exegetical corpus in respect to the Hebrew Scriptures and their translation, collections of stories about authorities, various kinds of sayings assigned to them -- an extraordinarily large mass of materials. Our approach, for the first time, must encompass the totality of the evidence, cope with, take account of, sources of exceptional density and richness. The law, as I said, is the definitive source of the world-view of the earlier rabbis. What is earliest and best attested is The Mishnah-Tosefta. Therefore, if we want to know what people were thinking in the first and second centuries, we have to turn, to begin with, to that document, which must serve as criterion in the assessment of whatever first appears in the later compilations of rabbinical sayings and stories. Books on rabbinic Judaism which focus upon non-legal sayings (without regard, even, to the time at which the documents containing those sayings were redacted) simply miss the point of rabbinic Judaism.

But the legal sayings deal with picayune and inconsequential matters. The major problem is to derive, from arcane and trivial details of laws of various sorts, the world-view which forms the foundations of, and is expressed by, these detailed rules. That work must be done in a systematic and comprehensive way. And, in consequence, the definition of the agendum of scholarship is to be revised, not merely in terms of the adaptation and systematic application of methods of literary-, form-, and redactional-criticism, hitherto unknown in this field, nor in terms of the introduction of historical-critical considerations, hitherto neglected or introduced in an episodic way and with a lack of historical sophistication, but in terms of its very shape and structure. The total failure of all prior approaches finds definitive illustration in Urbach's disastrous work. Critics of the old approaches could not have provided a better satire of the intellectual bankruptcy of the age that has gone before than does Urbach himself.

Still, Urbach presents the scholarly world with original scholarship. What of an effort to describe "Palestinian Judaism" in the first century out of the resources of the fourth, sixth, and tenth centuries? I refer to a work belonging in the same category as Moore and Urbach, but hardly of the same stature and quality, E. P. Sanders.[16] "Palestinian Judaism" is described through three bodies of evidence: Tannaitic literature, the Dead Sea Scrolls, and Apocrypha and Pseudepigrapha, in that order. The issue of category-formation obviously stands forth: how does Sanders knkow what categories to address to his chosen evidence -- and how does he choose his evidence? I shall deal only with how he treats the first oof the three bodies of sources under discussion. I find the work conceptually contemptible.

To each set of sources, Sanders addresses the same categories: specifically, questions of systematic theology: election and covenant, obedience and disobedience, reward and punishment and the world to come, salvation by membership in the covenant and atonement, proper religious behavior (so for Tannaitic sources); covenant and the covenant people, election and predestination, the commandments, fulfillment and transgression, atonement (Dead Sea Scrolls); election and covenant, the fate of the individual Israelite, atonement, commandments, the basis of salvation, the gentiles, repentance and atonement, the righteousness of God (Apocrypha and Pseudepigrapha, meaning, specifically: Ben Sira, I Enoch, Jubilees, Psalms of Solomon, IV Ezra). There follows a brief concluding chapter (pp. 419-28, summarizing pp. 1-418), and then the second part, on Paul, takes up about a fifth of the book. Sanders provides a very competent bibliography (pp. 557-82) and thorough indexes. So far as the book has a polemical charge, it is to demonstrate (pp. 420-21) that "the fundamental nature of the covenant conception... largely accounts for the relative scarcity of appearances of the term 'covenant' in Rabbinic literature. The covenant was presupposed, and the Rabbinic discussions were largely directed toward the question of how to fulfill the covenantal obligations." This proposition is then meant to disprove the conviction ("all but universally held") that Judaism is a degeneration of the Old Testament view: "The once noble idea of covenant as offered by God's grace and obedience as the consequence of that gracious gift degenerated into the idea of petty legalism, according to which one had to earn the mercy of God by minute observance of irrelevant ordinances."

---

[16] E. P. Sanders, *Paul and Palestinian Judaism. A Comparison of Patterns of Religion* (London: SCM Press, 1977). Pp. xviii+627.

Sanders' search for patterns yields a common pattern in "covenantal nomism," which, in general, emerges as follows (p. 422):

> The "pattern" or "structure" of covenantal nomism is this: (1) God has chosen Israel and (2) given the law. The law implies both (3) God's promise to maintain the election and (4) the requirement to obey. (5) God rewards obedience and punishes transgression. (6) The law provides for means of atonement, and atonement results in (7) maintenance or re-establishment of the covenantal relationship. (8) All those who are maintained in the covenant by obedience, atonement, and God's mercy belong to the group which will be saved. An important interpretation of the first and last points is that election and ultimately salvation are considered to be by God's mercy rather than human achievement.

Anyone familiar with Jewish liturgy will be at home in that statement. Even though the evidence on the character of Palestinian Judaism derives from diverse groups and reaches us through various means, Sanders argues that covenantal nomism was "the basic type of religion known by Jesus and presumably by Paul..." And again, "covenantal nomism must have been the general type of religion prevalent in Palestine before the destruction of the Temple."!2!

The stated purposes require attention. Sanders states at the outset (p. xii) that he has six aims: (1) to consider methodologically how to compare two (or more) related but different religions; (2) to destroy the view of Rabbinic Judaism which is still prevalent in much, perhaps most, New Testament scholarship; (3) to establish a different view of Rabbinic Judaism; (4) to argue a case concerning Palestinian Judaism (that is, Judaism as reflected in material of Palestinian provenance) as a whole; (5) to argue for a certain understanding of Paul; and (6) to carry out a comparison of Paul and Palestinian Judaism. Numbers (4) and (6), he immediately adds, "constitute the general aim of the book, while I hope to accomplish the others along the way." Since more than a third of the work is devoted to Rabbinic Judaism, Sanders certainly cannot be accused of treating his second goal casually.

Having described the overall shape of the work, let me make explicit the fact that this is a work of historical theology: *wissenschaftliche Theologie*. Sanders' very good intention nonetheless deserves the attention of students of religions who are not theologians, because what he wanted to achieve is in my view worthwhile. This intention is the proper comparison of religions (or of diverse expressions of one larger religion):

> "I am of the view... that the history of the comparison of Paul and Judaism is a particularly clear instance of the general need for methodological improvement in the comparative study of religion. What is difficult is to focus on what is to be compared. We have already seen that most comparisons are of reduced essences... or of individual motifs..."

This sort of comparison Sanders rejects. Here I wish to give Sanders' words, because I believe what he wants to do is precisely what he should have done but, as I shall explain, has not succeeded in doing:

> What is clearly desirable, then, is to compare an entire religion, parts and all, with an entire religion, parts and all; to use the analogy of a building to compare two buildings, not leaving out of account their individual bricks. The problem is how to discover two wholes, both of which are considered and defined on their own merits and in their own terms, to be compared with each other.

On the basis of my description of the contents of the book, we must conclude that he has not compared an entire religion, parts and all, with other such entire religions. For the issues of election and covenant, obedience and disobedience, and the like, while demonstrably present and taken for granted in the diverse "Judaisms" of late antiquity, do not necessarily define the generative problematic of any of the Judaisms before us. Sanders' principle of category-formation derives from Protestant theological concerns, not from the evidence of the Judaism that interedsts him. To put matters in more general terms: Systemic description must begin with the system to be described. Comparative description follows. And to describe a system, we commence with the principal documents which can be shown to form the center of a system. Our task then is to uncover the exegetical processes, the dynamics of the system, through which those documents serve to shape a conception, and to make sense, of reality. We then must locate the critical tensions and inner problematic of the system thereby revealed: What is it about? What are its points of insistence? The comparison of systems begins in their exegesis and interpretation.

But Sanders does not come to Rabbinic Judaism (to focus upon what clearly is his principal polemical charge) to uncover the issues of Rabbinic Judaism. He brings to the Rabbinic sources the issues of Pauline scholarship and Paul.!3! This blatant trait of his work, which begins, after all, with a long account of Christian anti-Judaism ("The persistence of the view of Rabbinic religion as one of legalistic works-righteousness," pp. 33-58), hardly requires amplification. In fact, Sanders does not really undertake the systemic description of earlier Rabbinic Judaism in terms of its critical tension. True, he isolates those documents he thinks may testify to the state of opinion in the late first and second centuries. But Sanders does not describe Rabbinic Judaism through the systemic categories yielded by its principal documents. His chief purpose is to demonstrate that Rabbinism constitutes a system of "covenantal nomism." While I think he is wholly correct in maintaining the importance of the conceptions of covenant and of grace, the polemic in behalf of Rabbinic legalism as covenantal does not bring to the fore what Rabbinic sources themselves wish to take as their principal theme and generative problem. For them, as he says, covenantal nomism is a datum. So far as Sanders proposes to demonstrate the importance to all the kinds of ancient Judaism of covenantal nomism, election, atonement, and the like, his work must be pronounced a success but trivial. So far as he claims to effect systemic description of Rabbinic Judaism ("a comparison of patterns of religion"), we have to evaluate that claim in its own terms.

My criticism at this point concerns how Sanders does what he has chosen to do: systemic comparison. His notion of comparing patterns of religion is, I believe, promising. But what he has done, instead, is to impose the pattern of one religious expression, Paul's, upon the description of another, that of the Tannaitic-Rabbinical sources. He therefore ignores the context of the sayings adduced in the service of comparison, paying little attention to the larger context in which those sayings find meaning. In this connection I point to the observation of Mary Boyce:[17]

> Zoroaster's eschatological teachings, with the individual judgment, the resurrection of the body, the Last Judgment, and life everlasting, became profoundly familiar, through borrowings, to Jews, Christians, and Muslims, and have exerted enormous influence on the lives and thoughts of men in many lands. Yet it was in the framework of his own faith that they attained their fullest logical coherence....

What Boyce stresses is that, taken out of the Zoroastrian context, these familiar teachings lose their "fullest logical coherence." Sanders, for his part, has not asked what is important and central in the system of Tannaitic-Rabbinic writtings. All he wants to know is what, in those writings, addresses questions of interest to Paul. In my judgment, even in 1973 he would have been better served by paying close attention to his own statement of purpose.

But since 1973 the state of the art has shifted its focus, from the mass of writings in which authorities of the first and second centuries (Tannaim, hence Tannaitic literature) are cited, to the character of the documents, one by one, which contain and express Rabbinic Judaism. That, after all, is the argument presented in this book: the centrality of the canon in all work of description. Future work of comparison, then, will have to take up the results of something less encompassing than "the Tannaitic view of...," all the more so, "the rabbinic idea of...." The work of description, first for its own purposes, then for systemic comparison, begins with the Mishnah.

The Mishnah certainly is the first document of Rabbinic Judaism. Formally, it stands at the center of the system, since the principal subsequent Rabbinic documents, the Talmuds, lay themselves out as if they were exegeses of the Mishnah (or, more accurately, of the Mishnah-Tosefta). It follows that an account of what the Mishnah is about, of the system expressed by the Mishnah and of the world-view created and sustained therein, should be required for

---

[17] *A History of Zoroastrianism* [Leiden, 1975], p. 246.

systemic comparison such as Sanders proposes. Now if we come to the Mishnah with questions of Pauline-Lutheran theology, important to Sanders and New Testament scholarship, we find ourselves on the peripheries of Mishnaic literature and its chief foci. True, The Mishnah contains a very few relevant, accessible sayings, for example, on election and covenant. But on our hands is a huge document which does not wish to tell us much about election and covenant and which does wish to speak about other things. Category-formation marks the difference: Sanders, like Urbach, following Moore, forms categories outside of the data -- pure anachronism, notr of a historica.l, but of a cultural and philosophical order.

Description of the Mishnaic system is not easy. It took me twenty-two volumes to deal with the sixth of the Mishnah's six divisions, and four of the otherfive divisions (excluding Agriculture) brought the project up to forty-three volumes. So it is quite a project. We cannot therefore blame Sanders for not doing what has only just now been undertaken. But we have to wonder whether Sanders has asked of himself the generative and unifying questions of the core of the Mishnah at all: Has he actually sat down and studied (not merely "read") one document, even one tractate, beginning to end, and analyzed its inner structure, heart, and center? By this question I do not mean to ask whether Sanders has mastered Rabbinic writings. The evidence in his book is that he can look things up, presumably with Billerbeck's help. He knows Hebrew and is competent, if not expert. The question is, Does Sanders so grasp the problematic of a Rabbinic compilation that he can accurately state what it is that said compilation wishes to express -- its generative problematic? Or does he come to the Rabbinic literature with a quite separate and distinct set of questions, issues in no way natural to, and originating in, the Rabbinic writings themselves? That is the heart of the issue of caegoiry-formation. Just now we noticed that Sanders' theological agendum accords quite felicitously with the issues of Pauline theology. To show that that agendum has not been shaped out of the issues of Rabbinic theology, I shall now adduce negative evidence on whether Sanders with equal care analyzes the inner structure of a document of Rabbinic Judaism.

First, throughout his "constructive" discussions of Rabbinic ideas about theology, Sanders quotes all documents equally with no effort at differentiation among them. He seems to have culled sayings from the diverse sources he has chosen and written them down on cards, which he proceeded to organize around his critical categories. Then he has constructed his paragraphs and sections by flipping through those cards and commenting on this and that. So there is no context in which a given saying is important in its own setting, in its own document. This is Billerbeck-scholarship, as modified by Urbach.

Of greater importance, the diverse documents of Rabbinism are accorded no attention on their own. Let me expain what I mean. Anyone who sits down and studies Sifra, in a large unit of its materials, for example, can hardly miss what the redactor of the document wants to say. The reason is that the polemic of that document is so powerfully stated and so interminably repeated as to be inescapable. What Sifra wishes to say is this: The Mishnah requires an exegetical foundation. But the Mishnah notoriously avoids scriptural proof-texts. To Sifra none of the Mishnah's major propositions is acceptable solely upon the basis of reason or logic. All of them require proper grounding in exegesis -- of a peculiarly formal sort -- of Scripture. One stratum of the Talmuds, moreover, addresses the same devastating critique to the Mishnah. For once a Mishnaic proposition will be cited at the head of a talmudic pericope, a recurrent question is, What is the source of this statement? And the natural and right answer (from the perspective of the redactor of this sort of pericope) will be, As it is said..., followed by a citation of Scripture.

Now if it is so that Sifra and at least one stratum of Talmud so shape their materials as to make a powerful polemical point against the Mishnah's autonomous authority ("logic"), indifferent as the Mishnah is to scriptural authority for its laws, then we must ask how we can ignore or neglect that polemic. Surely we cannot cite isolated pericopae of these documents with no attention whatsoever to the intention of the documents which provide said pericopae. Even the most primitive New Testament scholars will concur that we must pay attention to the larger purposes of the several evangelists in citing sayings assigned to Jesus in the various Gospels. Everyone knows that if we ignore Matthew's theory of the law and simply extract Matthew's versions of Jesus' sayings about the law and set them up side by side with the sayings about the law given to Jesus by other of the evangelists and attitudes imputed to him by Paul, we create a mess of contradictions. Why then should the context of diverse Rabbinic sayings, for example, on the law, be ignored? In this setting it is gratuitous to ask for an explanation of Sanders' constant reference to "the Rabbis," as though the century and a half which he claims to discuss produced no evidence of individuals' and ideas' having distinct histories. This is ignorant.

The diverse Rabbinic documents require study in their own terms. The systems of each -- so far as there are systems -- have to be uncovered and described. The way the several systems relate and the values common to all of them have to be spelled out. The notion that we may cite promiscuously everything in every document (within the defined canon of "permitted" documents) and then claim to have presented an account of "the Rabbis" and their opinions is not demonstrated and not even very well argued. We hardly need dwell on the still more telling fact that Sanders has not shown how systemic comparison is possible when, in point of fact, the issues of one document, or of one system of which a document is a part, are simply not the same as the issues of some other document or system. That is, he has succeeded in finding Rabbinic sayings on topics of central importance to Paul (or Pauline theology). He has not even asked whether these sayings form the center and core of the Rabbinic system or even of a given Rabbinic document. To state matters simply, How do we know that "the Rabbis" and Paul are talking about the same thing, so that we may compare what they have to say? And if it should turn out that "the Rabbis" and Paul are not talking about the same thing, then what is it that we have to compare?

Even by 1973 it was clear that the issue of historical dependability of attributions of sayings to particular rabbis had to be faced, even though, admittedly, it had not been faced in most of the work on which Sanders was able to draw. I do not wish to dwell upon the problem of why we should believe that a given rabbi really said what is attributed to him, because I have already discussed that matter at some length. Still, it seems to me that the issues of historical evidence should enter into the notion of the comparison of systems. If it should turn out that "the Rabbis'" ideas about a given theological topic respond to a historical situation subject to fairly precise description, then the work of comparison becomes still more subtle and precarious. For if "the Rabbis" address their thought -- for example, about the right motive for the right deed -- to a world in which, in the aftermath of a terrible catastrophe, the issue of what it is that human beings still control is central, the comparison of their thought to that of Paul requires us to imagine what Paul might have said if confronted by the situation facing "the Rabbis."

A powerful motif in sayings assigned to authorities who lived after the Bar Kokhba war is the issue of attitude: the surpassing power of human intention in defining a situation and judging it. In many ways diverse tractates of The Mishnah seem to want to say that there are yet important powers left in the hands of defeated, despairing Israelites. The message of much of Mishnaic halakhah is that there is an unseen world, a metaphysical world, subject to the will of Israel. Given the condition of defeat, the despair and helplessness of those who survived the end of time, we may hardly be surprised at the message of authorities who wish to specify important decisions yet to be made by people totally subjugated to the will of their conquerors. Now if we ignore that historical setting, the dissonances of theology and politics, in which the message concerning attitude and intention is given, how are we properly to interpret and compare "the Rabbis'" teachings on the effects of the human will with those of Paul, or those assigned to Jesus, for that matter? If they say the same thing, it may be for quite divergent reasons. If they say different things, it may be that they say different things because they speak of different problems to different people.

Now these observations seem to me to be obvious and banal. But they are necessary to establish the urgency of facing those simple historical questions Sanders wishes to finesse (by quoting me, of all people!). If we have a saying assigned to Aqiba how do we know it really was said by him, belonging to the late first and early second century? If we cannot show that it does go back to A.D. 100, then we are not justified in adducing such sayings as evidence of the state of mind of one late-first- and early-second-century authority, let alone of all the late-first- and early-second-century authorities -- and let alone of "the Rabbis" of the later first and whole of the second centuries. I cannot concede that Sanders' notion of systemic description, even if it were wholly effected, has removed from the critical agendum these simple questions of historical study we have yet to answer.

Nor should we ignore the importance in the work, not only of comparison, but also of interpreting a given saying, of establishing the historical context in which the saying was said (or at least in which it was important to be quoted). Sanders many times cites the famous saying attributed to Yohanan b. Zakkai that the corpse does not contaminate, nor does purification water purify, but the whole thing is hocus-pocus. That saying first occurs in a later, probably fourth-century, Midrashic compilation. Surely we might wonder whether, at the time of the making of that compilation, issues of magic were not central in Rabbinic discourse. The denial of efficacy, *ex opere operato*, of a scriptural purification rite, addressed to a world in which magic, including Torah magic, was deemed to work ex opere operato, may be interpreted as a powerful polemic against a strong current of the fourth-century Palestinian and Babylonian Jews' life, a time at which Rabbinical circles, among others, were deeply interested in the magical powers inherent in Torah. Now I do not mean to suggest that the proper interpretation of the saying is in accord with this hypothesis, nor do I even propose the stated hypothesis for serious consideration here. I only offer it as an example of one context in which the saying is credibly to be interpreted and, more important, as evidence of the centrality of context in the interpretation of each and every saying. If we do not know where and when a saying was said, how are we to interpret the saying and explain its meaning?

Establishing the correct categories dictates, also, the definition of the context of interpretation. In my view the meaning of a saying is defined, at the outset, by the context in which it is meaningful. To be sure, the saying may remain meaningful later on, so that, cited for other purposes, the saying takes on new meanings. No one denies that obvious proposition, which, after all, is illustrated best of all by the history of the interpretation, but, of greater systemic consequence, the deliberate misinterpretation, of the Old Testament in Judaism and Christianity. If that is so, then we surely should not reduce to a fundamentalistic and childish hermeneutical framework the interpretation by sayings attributed to rabbis in Rabbinic documents of diverse periods, put together, as I said earlier, for diverse purposes and therefore addressed, it seems to me self-evident, to historically diverse circumstances.

Since this is one of the most ambitious works in Pauline scholarship in twenty-five years and since, as I just said, it does adumbrate initiatives of considerable methodological promise, we must ask ourselves what has gone wrong with Sanders' immense project. I think the important faults are on the surface. Sanders has given us a good proposal on "the holistic comparison of patterns of religion" (pp. 12-24), then he should have tried to allow his book to unfold as an exposition and instantiation of his program of systemic comparison. This he does not do. His approach to the Rabbinic literature covers too much or too little (I am not sure which). That is, he begins with a sizable description of methodological problems. But when he comes to the substantive exposition of the Rabbinic theology important for his larger project, Sanders seems to me to have forgotten pretty much everything he said on method. There are acres and acres of paragraphs which in sum and substance could have been lifted straightaway from Schechter, Moore, or Urbach, to name three other efforts at systematic dogmatics in early Rabbinic religion. I found the systematic theology of the Dead Sea Scrolls equally tedious but know too little of the problems of working on those sources to suggest how things might have been done differently and better. But to produce Sanders' substantive results of the theological discussions, from election and covenant to the nature of religious life and experience (pp. 84-232), we simply do not need to be told about critical problems ("the use of Rabbinic material, the nature of Tannaitic literature") laid out earlier (pp. 59-83). In all, it seems to me a bit pretentious, measured against the result.

In regard to Rabbinic Judaism, Sanders' book also is so profoundly flawed as to be hopeless and, I regret to say it, useless in accomplishing its stated goals of systemic description and comparison. No, systems which have not been accurately described cannot be compared. And the work of description surely involves critical intiatives in selection and interpretation. But to take up the work of interpretation, to design a project of comparison and carry it through, to reckon with the complexities of diverse documents and systems -- these are essentially the tasks of our own exegesis of these ancient texts and systems. To effect the comparison of patterns of ancient Judaism, what is needed is our self-conscious exegesis of their unself-conscious exegesis. Ands for that purpose, we begin with a clear account of how we have defined our categories -- and justeified them against, and within, evidence. And that brings us to the conclusion of this book.

VIII

From "Judaism" to *Torah*

This brings us back after a sizable digression, to the contrary principle of category-formation, the one that commences with the sources, that is, the canon or the Torah. How do we proceed to form categories out of that principle of formation? One route to the interpretation of a system is to specify the sorts of issues it chooses to regard as problems, the matters it chooses for its close and continuing exegesis. When we know the things about which people worry, we have some insight into the way in which they see the world. So we ask, when we approach the canon of Judaism in late antiquity, about its critical tensions, the recurring issues which occupy its great minds. It is out of concern with this range of issues, and not some other, that the canon of Judaism in late antiquity defines its principal areas for discussion. Here is the point at which the great exercises of law and theology will be generated -- here and not somewhere else. This is a way in which we specify the choices people have made, the selections a system has effected. When we know what people have chosen, we also may speculate about the things they have rejected, the issues they regard as uninteresting or as closed. We then may describe the realm of thought and everyday life which they do not deem subject to tension and speculation. It is on these two sides -- the things people conceive to be dangerous and important, the things they set into the background as unimportant and uninteresting -- which provide us with a key to a Judaism -- that is to say, the culture of a community or, as I prefer to put it, to the system constructed and expressed by a given group of people.

The central issues, those questions which generate insight worth sharing and understanding worth having, therefore, are to be defined in these terms: What does the canon of Judaism in late antiquity, viewed by its components and then as a whole, define as its central problems? How does the canon of Judaism in late antiquity perceive the critical tensions of its world? We want to describe the solutions, resolutions, and remissions it poses for these tensions. We propose to unpack and then to put back together again the world-view of the canon as a whole, document by document. When we can explain how this system fits together and works, then we shall know something worth knowing., which is how to describe, analyze, and interpret *the Torah*.

Index